Harvard Business Review

ON

CEO SUCCESSION

D1595694

THE HARVARD BUSINESS REVIEW PAPERBACK SERIES

The series is designed to bring today's managers and professionals the fundamental information they need to stay competitive in a fast-moving world. From the preeminent thinkers whose work has defined an entire field to the rising stars who will redefine the way we think about business, here are the leading minds and landmark ideas that have established the *Harvard Business Review* as required reading for ambitious businesspeople in organizations around the globe.

Other books in the series:

Other books in the series (continued):

Other books in the series (continued):

Harvard Business Review on Managing Yourself

Harvard Business Review on Marketing

Harvard Business Review on Measuring Corporate Performance

Harvard Business Review on Mergers and Acquisitions

Harvard Business Review on the Mind of the Leader

Harvard Business Review on Motivating People

Harvard Business Review on Negotiation and Conflict Resolution

Harvard Business Review on Nonprofits

Harvard Business Review on Organizational Learning

Harvard Business Review on the Persuasive Leader

Harvard Business Review on Profiting from Green Business

Harvard Business Review on Strategic Alliances

Harvard Business Review on Strategic Renewal

Harvard Business Review on Strategic Sales Management

Harvard Business Review on Strategies for Growth

Harvard Business Review on Supply-Chain Management

Harvard Business Review on Talent Management

Harvard Business Review on Teams That Succeed

Harvard Business Review on the Tests of a Leader

Harvard Business Review on Top-Line Growth

Harvard Business Review on Turnarounds

Harvard Business Review on Women in Business

Harvard Business Review on Work and Life Balance

Harvard Business Review

ON

CEO SUCCESSION

A HARVARD BUSINESS REVIEW PAPERBACK

Library of Congress Cataloging-in-Publication Data

Harvard business review on CEO succession.
        p. cm
    Includes index.
    ISBN 978-1-4221-2869-5 (pbk.: alk. paper)
    1.   Executive succession. 2.   Executives—Selection and
appointment. 3.   Directors of corporations. 4.   Industrial
management. I.   Title: On CEO successsion.
    HD38.2.H37433 2009
    658.4'0711—dc22

                                            2009010451

Table of Contents

Harvard Business Review

ON

CEO SUCCESSION

The CEO's Real Legacy

Executive Summary

THE LITERATURE ON CEO SUCCESSION plan-
ning is nearly unanimous in its advice: Begin early,
look first inside your company for exceptional talent,
see that candidates gain experience in all aspects
of the business, and help them develop the skills
they will need in the top job. It all makes sense and
sounds pretty straightforward. Nevertheless, the list
of CEOs who last no more than a few years on the
job continues to grow. Implicit in many, if not all,
of these unceremonious departures is the absence
of an effective CEO succession plan.

The problem is, most boards simply don't want
to talk about CEO succession: Why rock the boat
when things are going well? Why risk offending
the current CEO? Meanwhile, most CEOs can't

imagine that anyone could adequately replace them.

In this article, Kenneth W. Freeman, the retired CEO of Quest Diagnostics, discusses his own handoff experience (Surya N. Mohapatra became chief executive in May 2004) and offers his approach to succession planning. He says it falls squarely on the incumbent CEO to put ego aside and initiate and actively manage the process of selecting and grooming a successor. Aggressive succession planning is one of the best ways for CEOs to ensure the long-term health of the company, he says. Plus, thinking early and often about a successor will likely improve the chief executive's performance during his tenure.

Freeman advocates the textbook rules for succession planning but adds to that list a few more that apply specifically to the incumbent CEO: Insist that the board become engaged in succession planning, look for a successor who is different from you, and make the successor's success your own. After all, Freeman argues, the CEO's true legacy is determined by what happens *after* he leaves the corner office.

T HE LITERATURE ON CEO SUCCESSION planning is nearly unanimous in its advice: Begin early, look first inside your company for exceptional talent, see that candidates gain experience in all aspects of the business, help them develop the skills they'll need in the top job. It all makes sense and sounds pretty straightforward.

Nevertheless, the list of companies with CEOs who last no more than a few years after taking the reins continues to grow. No need to rattle off the names here—they're known to any casual reader of business publications. But we can draw a conclusion from this parade of chief executives marching out the door: Implicit in many, if not all, of these unceremonious departures is the absence of an effective CEO succession plan.

Anyone would think this discouraging track record—not to mention the increased regulatory pressure on corporate boards to play a more active governance role—would spur directors to take steps to avoid similar disappointments at their own companies. But during good times, most boards simply don't want to talk about CEO succession. Why rock the boat when things are going well? Why offend an incumbent CEO who is doing a great job? Why take valuable board time to discuss a succession that is unlikely to occur for years? During bad times, when the board is ready to fire the CEO, it's too late to talk about a plan for smoothly passing the baton.

So if boards aren't likely to take responsibility for succession planning, who should? The answer is obvious: the current CEO. Early—and I mean early—in your tenure as CEO, you should initiate and then actively manage the process of selecting and grooming a successor. You should follow the textbook rules: Identify the best talent, combine strategic planning with leadership development, and work closely with the chosen successor to ensure a seamless transition. But these principles should be expanded to include a few that the management literature overlooks—principles that apply specifically to the incumbent CEO.

One reason for you to take the lead in managing the succession process—and, if necessary, to prod the board to collaborate with you—is the unfortunate possibility that your term may be cut short by illness or accident. More important, aggressive succession planning is one of the best ways for you to ensure the long-term health of your company. There is one other, somewhat counter-intuitive benefit: Thinking early and often about a successor will likely improve your performance during your time in the position.

Dealing with the Big E

Before we get to my own recent handoff at Quest Diagnostics, let's take a look at one of the biggest barriers to adopting the succession approach I am advocating—the CEO ego.

It's no secret that few chief executives are in any hurry to bring up the topic of succession. Most of them, justifiably or not, believe their own laudatory press. They can't imagine that an adequate replacement exists. Whatever the validity of these perceptions, most CEOs are understandably loath to give up the power, perks, and prestige that the boss enjoys. Consequently, they stay in their jobs too long. I know a company in which the chairman and CEO brought in a chief operating officer as his heir apparent—and then fired him. He brought in another COO—and fired him, as well. When the third COO joined the company, the board had to say to the chairman, "This one is going to become the CEO."

I've long been committed to the notion of CEO term limits for reasons that relate both to the organization and to the individual. Companies and individuals achieve greatness when they embrace change, taking risks to move to the next level. Occasionally, a CEO can continually reinvent both himself and his organization; most often, though, the CEO's actions become predictable over time. The company gets comfortable with the status quo, and the organization's ability to change is severely diminished. I've come to realize that it's better to give your all during the finite time your leadership is still fresh and people are still on their toes. Furthermore, knowing that your days are numbered injects a sense of urgency into your work.

But there's another reason that a CEO shouldn't view his or her job as a permanent position. As the issues facing a business evolve, the CEO must also evolve. At some point, though, evolution isn't enough: The chief executive's talents will no longer be matched to the strategic challenges facing the company. At this stage—or, even better, before it—the CEO should yield to someone with skills better suited to the issues at hand. Even here, the ego problem can rear its ugly head. I think it is safe to say that some CEOs are so attached to the prestige they have enjoyed in their leadership roles that they secretly hope to see their successors stumble, thereby making their own achievements look better in retrospect.

Well, I don't think I was guilty of secretly harboring that perverse emotion. But let me tell you that my ego, too, knows how difficult it is to let go of the helm. One day I had 37,000 employees looking to me for direction, depending on me for their paychecks. The next day I woke up, and those 37,000 people were looking to someone else. It's hard not to feel like your identity is being stripped away when you relinquish the CEO title. I experienced that acutely this past spring when *BusinessWeek* was putting together its annual ranking of corporate America's 50 best-performing companies, right around the time that Surya N. Mohapatra was preparing to take over from me as CEO. Quest Diagnostics was ranked 34, and though I can't say I'm proud to admit it, I wanted my picture to accompany the business profile in the magazine. Luckily for me, the article appeared before the transition. Although I was prepared to accept my place out of the spotlight, I would have been disappointed to do so.

Keeping your ego in check through the discipline of managing your succession yields a benefit more immediate than the long-term health of the company: It can make you a better CEO. While you're thinking about the skills your successor will need, you'll also be dispassionately evaluating your own strengths and limitations. You may even identify organizational problems that, because of your temperament or talents, you aren't currently tackling. Whether you take these on or decide they are best left to a successor, the very act of thinking in this way provides you with a particularly clear-eyed view of the company and its challenges.

Anyway, as someone aware of his own ego, I tried from the beginning to avoid the usual mistakes CEOs make in succession planning. At the risk of falling into another ego trap—the unwarranted assumption that my approach is a blueprint for succession success—let me say that I think my experience offers a useful perspective on the process. Perhaps the most important lesson, one that even my own ego can endorse: Your true legacy as a CEO is what happens to the company *after* you leave the corner office.

From Survival to Evolution

I stepped down as CEO of Quest Diagnostics in May 2004 after nearly nine years in the job. My own route to the chief executive's office ran through Corning Incorporated, where, beginning in 1972, I held numerous financial and general management positions. In 1995, I joined Corning Clinical Laboratories, the predecessor company to Quest Diagnostics, as CEO. Quest Diagnostics performs medical tests on patients' blood and other specimens to help doctors diagnose and treat everything from cardiovascular disease to cystic fibrosis. When the company was spun off to Corning shareholders at the end of 1996, I became chairman and CEO. I took the job vowing to live up to my good intention not to linger too long. I couldn't imagine staying in the position for more than eight to ten years. But sticking to my guns was harder than I had imagined.

During my early days as CEO, succession planning wasn't near the top of anyone's agenda. The board and senior management team had their hands full just trying to save the company. The business had made several major acquisitions in 1993 and 1994, and it was facing some serious integration challenges and a heavy debt load. One of the acquired companies was accused of Medicare fraud, which ultimately led to a $100 million settlement with the government. We were also trying to stem the flight of physician groups and hospitals that were unhappy with the quality of our service and dealing with the downward slide in prices caused by overcapacity in the industry and competition for big managed-care contracts. Quest Diagnostics was in survival mode.

Nonetheless, because of my views on CEO tenure, I forced myself almost from the beginning to think about possible candidates to succeed me. First, I carefully considered people inside the company. There were some wonderful people on the senior team, but I quickly concluded that none of them possessed the unique attributes that the business would need in the future. In many ways, the strengths of the best internal candidates mirrored mine. Though I lacked experience in the health care industry, I did know operations and finance. And that was the functional expertise we would need to achieve our first goal, surviving, and our second, becoming the leader in our industry by improving quality and forcing industry consolidation. The team I had was perfect for trying to meet those goals. But once we achieved them, we would need a different set of leadership skills to help us meet the next wave of challenges.

To drive improvements in quality and to create a common culture, we embarked on an aggressive Six Sigma program that focused on such areas as increasing the accuracy and turnaround times of our tests. After we had stabilized the company and achieved marginal profitability, we once again turned to acquisitions to fuel our growth, taking particular care to integrate an acquired company before embarking on another major deal. With the $1.3 billion acquisition in 1999 of our biggest competitor, SmithKline Beecham Clinical Laboratories, Quest Diagnostics more than doubled its revenue and became the leading provider of diagnostic testing, information, and services in the United States. Last year, the company had earnings of about $436 million on revenue of $4.7 billion. Quest Diagnostics performs testing on behalf of more than 130 million patients a year—managing, arguably, more clinical encounters than any other health care services company in the United States.

The majority of the company's rapid growth historically had come from acquisitions. But it was clear we also needed to move in directions that would allow us to capitalize on advances in medicine, science, and information technology. For example, cutting-edge procedures—such as gene-based and other highly sophisticated tests—

generate only about 20% of our revenues, but they are highly profitable and a vital part of the company's future. With this necessary evolution in mind, I began to think more actively about the kind of successor who would be best suited to that future, knowing that the right person did not exist inside the company. I was 48 years old and had been CEO just over three years.

We cast our net widely and settled on several candidates, including Surya, who was then a senior vice president and a member of the executive committee at Picker International, a manufacturer of advanced medical-imaging technologies (now part of Philips Medical Systems). After an exhaustive due diligence and interview process—including seven conversations with me—Surya joined Quest Diagnostics in February 1999 as senior vice president and chief operating officer. His medical and scientific knowledge—he holds an undergraduate degree in electrical engineering, a master's degree in medical electronics, and a doctorate in medical physics—and 20 years of broad experience in the health care industry were just the right credentials for the job. Four months later, he was named president.

With the aim of weighing the relative strengths and weaknesses of two potential successors, we did consider another candidate who came to us through an acquisition. The fit with this candidate just wasn't right. Surya, meanwhile, clicked with the business from day one. He understood the bigger health care issues, and he had a keen appreciation for the importance of providing exceptional care for patients. For five years, Surya and I worked together with an eye toward him succeeding me if his performance merited it. In that period, the board's assessment of Surya shifted from "he might" to "he could" to "he should" to "he will" become CEO.

During his apprenticeship, Surya had two jobs. One was to help manage the business, including the integration of SmithKline Beecham and the development of new sources of growth based on science and research rather than acquisitions. The other was to learn the leadership skills necessary to be CEO. He was a master of the content side of the new business—but there were some areas for improvement on the leadership side.

Will Surya be successful? Time will tell. He took over as CEO in May, and he will succeed me as chairman next month. One thing is clear: The board and I are confident that he is the right CEO at the right time for Quest Diagnostics. I've had my day at the company. This new frontier—the convergence of diagnostic testing, diagnostic imaging, and advances in information technology for medicine—will be Surya's to explore. If, as we expect, he proves to be a terrific success, it will be due in part to several principles that helped drive the process by which he became CEO.

Force the Board to Pay Attention

When I first raised the issue of succession with the board at Quest Diagnostics, its initial response was, without exaggerating too much, one of wonder. The directors were generally encouraged by my performance and appeared comfortable with my serving as CEO for as long as I wanted.

Certainly, the cozy relationships that some CEOs have with their directors can exacerbate boards' natural tendency to shy away from the issue of CEO succession. In my case, though, this was not a group of people with whom I had longstanding personal ties. In fact, it was a very independent bunch—proof, if any was needed, of the importance of a CEO's initiating the discussion about his own succession.

Even as the process moved forward over the years, I had to work to keep the issue front and center with the board. And when it was clear to me that Surya was the right person to take my place, I tried to facilitate a process through which directors would become as comfortable with him as I was.

Surya, like many scientists, was a bit reserved. Partly because of his cultural background, he also was instinctively respectful, if not deferential, to board members, whom he rightly viewed as his ultimate bosses. I could see that I needed to articulate for the board, which was used to my more outgoing style, that Surya was bringing something different to the table. I encouraged Surya to think of the directors as colleagues as well as superiors, and I suggested that he systematically schedule one-on-one meetings with them, which he did. A year before Surya formally joined the board in the fall of 2002, I changed a few things in the way meetings were conducted. I mixed up the seating chart, for example, so that Surya was sitting among the board members and not at the head of the table. And I started leaving the room when Surya was making presentations to encourage more informal and unfiltered interactions between him and the board members.

Over time, Surya became more assertive in his boardroom dealings, and the directors took more ownership of the succession process. In retrospect, I wish I'd engaged the board even earlier in the process of getting to know Surya and evaluating whether he was the right person for the job.

Look for Differences

As I have said, it was clear to me that Quest Diagnostics
needed a new kind of CEO if the company was to be successful in its next stage of growth. I don't think that's
unusual. At most companies, if a CEO has accomplished
what he set out to do, the company's needs will have
changed, and the successor will require different skills
and experience, as well as a different personality.

Finding such a person won't happen automatically. In
the hiring process, we all tend to choose the people who
most resemble us. But instead of looking in the mirror
for the essential characteristics of a successor, we should
look out the window toward the real future of the company and let that guide our choice.

Surya and I are very different people. He is introspec-
tive; I am outgoing. He grew up in rural India; I am from
the suburbs of New York City. I have an MBA; he has a
PhD. The most relevant difference, though, relates to our
professional skills. Surya's background is heavily—and
impressively—scientific. He not only is steeped in the
worlds of science and engineering but also has written
about and holds a number of patents in the areas of the
human cardiovascular system and magnetic resonance
imaging.

If Surya is about science, I am more about the arts.
One semester of physics in college was enough for me.
Music was my passion; for a short time, I wanted to
become a professional musician, making my living at the
keyboard. But I also wanted to eat, and I soon decided to
pursue a career at Corning on the financial side of things.

I recognized that given the way the diagnostic-testing
industry was changing, if I stayed on as CEO for another
four or five years I'd lack some crucial skills needed for

success in the job. I had to be honest with myself. If future strategic discussions involved the latest innovations in genetics or proteomics rather than the next acquisition, I not only wouldn't bring much to the table but I also wouldn't feel the necessary fire in my belly to implement our strategy.

All that being said, Surya and I did share one key characteristic: a fierce determination—and proven capability—to deliver strong business results.

Make Your Successor's Success Your Own

Unfortunately, a new CEO with a different style and different skills can find it hard to get out from under his predecessor's shadow—a shadow that the organization may find familiar and comforting. In such a case, the incumbent must make a serious commitment to help his successor step into his new role. With this in mind, I worked closely with Surya in the years before he became CEO, exploring with him the nature of our business and offering advice on matters that I thought would make him a stronger leader.

Our main forum for this was a Sunday afternoon phone call, an hour or so long, which we had at 4 PM nearly every week for five years. (We were disciplined in keeping this appointment—and missed more than a few tempting football games and concerts because of it!) Although our offices were right next to each other, there never seemed to be time during the week for this kind of uninterrupted conversation, one that mixed coaching, advice, and a mutual exchange of ideas.

During the calls, we covered everything from acquisition negotiations to scientific developments, from the Six Sigma program to personnel planning, from the highest-level strategic issues to how each other's families were doing. We'd each bring two or three things to discuss. In my case, these would often involve management skills I thought Surya needed to work on in order to enhance his existing strengths. The feedback I gave Surya on his performance and leadership skills was the kind that could come only from someone who saw him in action at close range—and who was rooting for his success. The advice could get very granular.

During Surya's first week on the job, he and I visited a lab in Baltimore, where I conducted a "town meeting" with the employees and roamed through the lab greeting everyone individually at their work areas—doing the sort of thing that comes naturally to me. Afterward, Surya, ever the reticent scientist, said, "I could never do that." My instantaneous reply was, "If you want to be CEO someday, you'll have to." So I suggested he get some coaching to develop his communications skills and, over the years, pushed him to test his new skills in public meetings with employees and investors.

We'd also use the phone conversations to talk about setting priorities and making decisions. Someone with a scientific bent is always in search of ever more information that will ultimately lead to the right answer. But in business, often what you need is *an* answer. I like to joke that Surya can get to "know" in his sleep; my job was to help him get to "no" at work. I remember a conversation when I said something like, "We've been talking about this personnel issue in Atlanta for the last four weeks. When are we going to do something? And what are we going to do?"

I don't mean to sound patronizing. If someone were providing me with detailed advice on my management style—indeed, if it were Surya himself doing so—that person could easily find similar areas for improvement. And though our meetings never involved lengthy critiques of me, the tables did begin to turn over the years. One Sunday afternoon, we were talking about a relatively small acquisition in the medical IT area that Surya had been pushing us to make. I saw it as a distraction; he saw it as a foothold in an area that offered significant potential. He persistently made his case—just as I had persistently prodded him to work on some of his management skills. In a very deliberate and forceful manner, he convinced me it was the right move to make.

Over time, Surya became more assertive not only with me but with the board. He became a polished and confident speaker. He was able to make decisions based on the crucial—even if not comprehensive—information.

Would our mentoring relationship have worked if the personal chemistry had been different? Our exchanges were full of candor and sometimes sharp disagreements, but Surya was an eager and ambitious learner, which allowed me to play in my own power alley as a coach. It certainly is possible that someone else might have bristled at what I felt was well-intentioned guidance. But I believe that, as long as there is mutual trust and respect, two people in this situation can find a comfort zone that will allow an incumbent to increase the successor's chances of success.

Don't Drag Your Feet

I was 53 years old when I stepped down as CEO of Quest Diagnostics. If I were 63 and had only a couple of years to go until retirement, maybe I would have stayed on. But then there would have been the risk that, when I turned 65, the board would have extended my contract for another three years and, as so often happens with a CEO, I'd have become a predictable part of the furniture.

There's a lot to be said for leaving at the top of your game. I often think of Sandy Koufax, the former Los Angeles Dodgers pitcher. Unlike many other all-star players who stayed on long past their primes—adding a coda of sadly failing skills to some of the greatest careers of all time—Koufax left baseball when he was still the best pitcher in either league. I like to think that I, too, stepped down at the right time.

Even if your skills are no longer ideal for a particular company, they are still highly valuable. I plan on embarking on a second career, running another organization, possibly even in an arena other than business, where my skills can provide value.

I should mention one other risk facing CEOs: the return appearance. With increasing regularity, executives are being called back by their former companies to resume the chief executive's job. But think twice before you do it. It means not only that your successor failed, but that you did, too—at succession planning.

Originally published in November 2004
Reprint R0411B

Holes at the Top

Why CEO Firings Backfire

MARGARETHE WIERSEMA

Executive Summary

WHEN A COMPANY does well, its CEO is showered with money and adulation. When it does poorly, the CEO gets the blame—and the boot. For better or worse, investors now view chief executives as the primary determinant of corporate performance. But the reality is that most companies perform no better after they dismiss their CEOs than they did in the years leading up to the dismissals. Worse, the organizational disruption created by a rushed firing can leave a company with deep and lasting scars. Far from being a silver bullet, the replacement of a CEO often amounts to little more than a self-inflicted wound.

The blame for such poor results, the author argues, lies squarely with boards of directors.

17

Boards often lack the strategic understanding of the business necessary to give due diligence to choosing a replacement CEO. Concern over restoring investor confidence quickly—rather than doing what's right for the company—drives the selection process. And all too often, companies continue to be dogged by the same old problems after the new CEOs come on board.

But a good board can make a CEO replacement pay off if its members first develop a better understanding of the business context, worry less about pleasing the investment community and more about a replacement's strategic fit, and take an active role in overseeing the new CEO and the performance and direction of the company. In the long run, such approaches are likely to foster stability at the helm—making it less likely a company will have to fire its CEO in the first place.

IN THE SPRING OF 1995, Kmart was struggling. Once the largest U.S. retailer, the company had been steadily losing ground to Wal-Mart and other competitors. After posting record sales and profits in 1992, it had experienced eight consecutive quarters of disappointing earnings, and its stock price had dropped 74%. Reacting to relentless pressure from shareholders, the company's board of directors dismissed the CEO, company veteran Joseph Antonini, and with great fanfare brought in outsider Floyd Hall to replace him. The arrival of Hall, a former executive at Target and Grand Union, cheered Wall Street, and the company's beleaguered stock shot up 8%. But the cheering was to prove short-lived. Kmart's

downward slide soon resumed, its stock price began to
slip further, and in 2000, Hall was replaced with Charles
Conaway, another outsider. Less than two years later, the
company filed for bankruptcy.

Kmart is an extreme case, but the situation is not an
unusual one. The firing of CEOs when performance nose-
dives has become commonplace in U.S. business. And it's
not hard to understand why. At a time when companies
have come to be judged by the valuation of their stock,
investors now view chief executives as the primary determinant of corporate performance. When companies do
well, their CEOs are showered with money, perks, and
adulation. When they do poorly, they're given the
blame—and the boot. The roster of recently deposed U.S.
CEOs is long and growing, including—in addition to
Kmart's Antonini and Hall—such names as Coca Cola's
Douglas Ivester, Ford's Jacques Nasser, and Procter &
Gamble's Durk Jager. And the trend is now spreading to
Europe as well, with high-profile dismissals at Deutsche
Telekom, ABB, Swiss Life, Fiat, Vivendi, and Bertels-
mann, among others.

But does firing a CEO pay off, or do most companies
end up like Kmart, with little or nothing to show for
bringing in a new leader? I've been studying that question over the last few years, and what I've found is not
encouraging. Most companies perform no better—in
terms of earnings or stock-price performance—after they
dismiss their CEOs than they did in the years leading up
to the dismissals. Worse, the organizational disruption
created by rushed firings—particularly the bypassing of
normal succession processes—can leave companies with
deep and lasting scars. Far from being a silver bullet, the
replacement of a CEO often amounts to little more than
a self-inflicted wound.

The blame for the poor results, my research indicates, lies squarely with boards of directors. Boards often lack the strategic understanding of the business necessary to give due diligence to the CEO selection process. Consequently, they rely too heavily on executive search firms, which are even less informed about the business than they are. Concern over restoring investor confidence quickly—rather than doing what's right for the company—drives the selection process. And board members' ignorance about the factors that drive company performance undermines their ability to provide strategic oversight after the CEO is dismissed. While boards have become accustomed to firing CEOs, they have not yet become adept at making the dismissals pay off.

The Numbers

Typically a CEO gets fired not because the board has thoughtfully and deliberately concluded that it's time for a change at the top but because investors, concerned about poor performance, demand a change. Board members, who have little idea how to address the underlying problems that got their company into trouble in the first place, seek to appease investors in the short term by handing them the CEO's head on a platter. But firing a CEO is not just a bad solution to a complex, long-term problem. It is also surprisingly ineffective at generating short-term gains.

In my research, I examined all instances of CEO turnover in the 500 largest public companies in the United States during 1997 and 1998. I divided the 83 successions that took place in those two years into three categories—outright dismissal, early retirement, and routine retirement—based on press coverage of the event. Of the 83 successions, 37% were dismissals, 34% were early retirements, and only 29% were routine retirements, occurring because the CEO had reached the mandatory retirement age. Given that "early retirement" is almost always a euphemism for a forced removal from office, as many as 71% of the departures can be considered involuntary—a striking change from traditional practice. Research from the 1980s indicates that the percentage of CEO departures not accounted for by normal, age-related retirements ranged from 13% to 36%.

In another break from tradition, I found that outsiders were brought in to replace CEOs 36% of the time. That's far higher than the 11% to 15% levels of outsider appointments found in studies of succession from the 1970s and early 1980s. And when it came to replacing dismissed as opposed to retiring CEOs, companies chose outsiders a whopping 61%, of the time.

So what was the result of all this turnover? Not much, as it turns out. I analyzed the financial performance of companies that had fired their CEOs in three ways. First, I compared company performance in the two years prior to CEO dismissal with performance two years after. Second, I compared performance with industry averages for the same periods. Finally, I compared the performance of companies that had fired their CEOs with the performance of those whose CEOs had retired. I found that companies with CEO dismissals experienced no significant improvement in their operating earnings or their stock performance. Operating earnings (earnings before interest and taxes) as a percentage of total assets averaged 11.2% before dismissal and 11.8% after dismissal—not a statistically significant difference. Return on assets averaged 2.6% before dismissal and 2.4% after, again not statistically significant. Company performance relative to industry average also failed to improve significantly after bringing in a new CEO. And performance lagged behind that of companies with routine CEO successions. I couldn't find a single measure suggesting that CEO dismissals have a positive effect on corporate performance. (I should note that both outgoing and incoming CEOs can manipulate earnings numbers. The incumbent may cut discretionary expenditures to boost reported earnings; the new CEO may decrease transition-year earnings, hoping to boost future earnings. In both cases, the time frame I used is long enough that those manipulations should be inconsequential.) A summary of the comparisons appears in the exhibit "How CEO Dismissals Affect Company Performance."

How CEO Dismissals Affect Company Performance

When performance sags, boards all too often succumb to investor pressure and fire their CEOs, looking for quick gains in earnings or stock-price returns. But as these charts show, company performance following these high-profile dismissals is almost always disappointing.

Company Performance Before and After CEO Firing (top graph)

Investors today view chief executives as the primary determinant of company performance, yet most companies perform no better after they fire their CEOs than they did in the years leading up to the dismissals.

Company Performance After CEO Firing Versus Routine Succession (bottom graph)

Companies that fire their CEOs not only fail to boost their earnings, they also do worse than companies that replace their CEOs in a routine succession process.

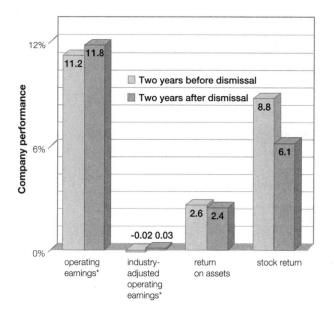

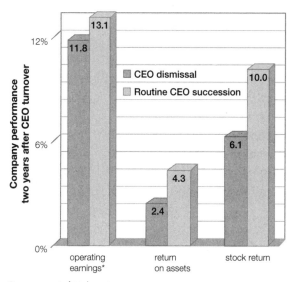

*as a percent of total assets

One company from my study, AT&T, is a case in point. In October 1997, the board dismissed Robert Allen, a 40-year company veteran, and brought in a celebrated outsider, former Hughes Electronics executive Michael Armstrong. Analysts' expectations of a turnaround under the charismatic Armstrong led initially to a near doubling of the company's stock price, from $47 to $90. However, Armstrong had inherited a company that was overly dependent on its core long-distance business and faced significant competitive and technological threats. The company was under pressure to generate earnings growth by pursuing alternative market opportunities to supplant the core business. Unfavorable market dynamics and the costly aftermath of Armstrong's strategy resulted in a steep decline in shareholder wealth. AT&T's share price plummeted, and earnings per share went from $2.44 in 1997 to $0.89 in 2001.

Doomed to Fail?

The firing of a CEO is a traumatic event in the life of any company. For it to be successful, the board of directors has to guide the process with skill and assurance. Unfortunately, that rarely happens. Most boards fail to provide the leadership required—and that, as much as anything else, accounts for the poor results of CEO dismissals. In examining the experiences of the companies in my study, I uncovered four reasons why boards' actions—or inactions—doom most dismissals to failure.

THE DISMISSAL SETS OFF A CRISIS

Attuned to the lack of investor confidence in the company's leadership, many boards take the path of least resistance and dismiss their CEOs. But the pressure doesn't stop there. The investment community wants a replacement CEO who's both promising and reassuring—and they want him fast.

Because board members are reacting to external pressure, they don't take the time to plan next steps before the dismissal occurs. And they find, after the dismissal, that the corporate organization is completely unable to help them identify a successor. Most large companies do have a reasonable executive succession-planning process in place—but it has one fatal flaw. The process is controlled and orchestrated by the incumbent CEO, which means that it's utterly useless if that CEO has just been fired. Extraordinary though this might sound, given how often CEOs are dismissed, boards don't take an active role in normal CEO succession planning, and companies don't make backup succession plans that acknowledge the possibility of an abrupt dismissal.

Suddenly, the directors have a big job to do all by themselves—a job that they have neither the time nor the expertise to do well. Board members usually hold demanding positions elsewhere; more than half are CEOs themselves. Nobody's able to make the search process into a full-time effort. The board, knowing that the investment community lacks patience, feels pressure to choose a replacement within three or four months. Typically, they turn the job over to an executive search firm. That would be a reasonable thing to do if the board were prepared to advise recruiters about the unique circumstances in which the company finds itself. Unfortunately, very few board members are able to give recruiters that kind of advice—which is the second reason most CEO firings and replacements are doomed to fail.

THE BOARD ISN'T EQUIPPED TO COPE WITH THE CRISIS

The sad fact is that few board members fully understand the businesses they supposedly oversee. In good times, they attend quarterly meetings, absorb the reports that the CEO prepares, give their approval to strategic initiatives, and leave. The CEO screens all the information they receive and controls the meeting agenda, which means that board members are unaware of many of the complex challenges the company faces and lack sufficient information to actively question the firm's direction or performance. Many critical decisions are never aired before the board. Directors rarely hear about the fierce disagreements over strategic direction that take place among members of the management team, for example; they hear only what the CEO wants them to hear after the disagreements have been resolved.

Because board members don't have a detailed understanding of the fundamental problems underlying the company's competitive deterioration, they can give a search firm only vague advice about what's needed in a new CEO. Essentially, they throw the job over the wall and wait to find out who's available and interested. The search firm, lacking direction in identifying the attributes an executive must have to turn the company around, brings in candidates who have been successful in the past but may have no particular knowledge of the company's industry or competitive situation. The board members don't see any problems with the candidates because they don't have any particular attributes in mind themselves. Indeed, at this stage they're not even thinking very clearly about what the company needs—and that's the third problem.

INVESTORS' CONCERNS DRIVE CEO SELECTION

Boards typically pay more attention to pleasing the investment community than they do to fixing the company during the CEO selection process. Analysts' stock valuations are driven in part by their confidence in the CEO. It's natural for board members to want to restore confidence—and stock prices—by appointing a CEO who will appeal to investors.

The desire to please (or appease) the investment community leads board members to choose a candidate who promises a quick fix, usually an outsider they hope will magically turn the company around. They barely consider internal candidates, partly because the investment community likes it that way, partly because any insider is, in a sense, guilty by association. The investment community welcomes the outsider, who supposedly represents a break with the past, by temporarily pushing up the company's stock price. The recent appointment of outsider Richard Notebaert as CEO of Qwest, for example, resulted in a 20% increase in the value of the stock in one day.

But external candidates are often less likely than insiders to understand the company's problems. Consider the case of George Fisher, who became CEO of Kodak in 1993 after Kay Whitmore was dismissed because of financial concerns. Fisher, the former Motorola chairman, adopted a growth strategy and invested heavily in new technology markets—mainly digital photography—while divesting noncore assets. Investors, assuming that Fisher's strategy would pay off, pushed up the stock price and P/E ratio. The company's actual operating earnings improved only slightly, however. Meanwhile, in its core film business—which still represented 80% of sales—Kodak was the high-cost producer despite considerable scale advantages. Fisher stayed focused on his strategy of growth through technology and put almost no pressure on manufacturing plants to improve efficiency. Fuji, Kodak's main competitor in this market, successfully launched an aggressive, price-based attack. The profitability of the core film business was seriously eroded—and Fisher's strategy of expanding the technological base never did result in the contribution to sales and earnings that he'd hoped for. Fisher's experience in the growth-oriented, technology-driven world of cell phones, pagers, and semiconductors made him ill-suited to the mature and increasingly cost-pressured business of photographic film.

BOARDS FAIL TO UNDERSTAND WHICH ISSUES DRIVE PERFORMANCE

Poorly performing companies don't get that way because of any single decision or for that matter any single leader. Patterns of historical decisions, strategic neglect, and misallocation of resources all contribute to the deterioration in performance; some contributing factors may even lie outside the company's control. Board members rarely have a deep understanding of those patterns and forces, which means that they can't provide sufficient oversight going forward or effectively evaluate the performance of the replacement CEO.

Toys R Us exemplifies the difficulty of turning around a deteriorating competitive position without first analyzing the underlying causes. When Robert Nakasone was thrust into the CEO role in 1998, replacing incumbent

Michael Goldstein, he took over a company facing several major threats to its profitability and viability. The market it had once monopolized was under direct attack by the discount retailers. In the 1990s, Wal-Mart, which had historically avoided the low-margin toy business, started to aggressively promote the most popular toys as loss leaders to build traffic. Not only that, technology had transformed the nature of toys and entertainment for the older-child market. Computers and electronic games had become toy substitutes, markets in which Toys R Us did not compete. As a result, the company's core toy business was shrinking and becoming ever less lucrative: Market share declined from 25.4% in 1990 to 16.8% in 1998.

Nakasone was under considerable pressure from the board to show that the company was on the right track. As CEO, he undertook significant cost reductions by closing underperforming stores, slashing inventories, and cutting the workforce to improve earnings. His operational improvements, however, did not solve the company's fundamental problems: new competitors in the toy business and technological substitution of toys. Unable to stem further declines in the company's competitive position and faced with a 45% stock price decline during his 18-month tenure, Nakasone, too, was forced out. Because the board was blind to the real challenges facing Toys R Us, it was unable to provide the strategic direction necessary to reap any benefits from new leadership.

A Blueprint for Success

Although many companies fail when it comes to replacing a CEO, not all do. Boards that manage the task effectively tend to have three things in common: They understand that selecting a CEO is a major responsibility, one that's theirs alone; they help the CEO set realistic performance expectations; and they develop a deep understanding of the company's strategic position.

TAKE THE RESPONSIBILITY SERIOUSLY

During the succession process, the board should let strategic needs dictate selection criteria for the new CEO. That's not always easy to do; board members have a tendency to become star-struck. This happens partly because they're trying to please the investment community, but it also happens because they, like investors, imagine that an outsider's charisma or past experience will trump his lack of knowledge about the company or the industry. To circumvent this problem, smart boards first identify the market, competitive, and technological factors that influence the company's performance. If members keep these factors in mind, they'll be better able to identify the skills and experiences that the new CEO will need.

Home Depot's recent CEO replacement process provides a good example of how this should be done. Ken Langone, the board's lead director, was acutely aware that the market and business had evolved in important ways. After two decades of spectacular growth, the company had reached a plateau. Big-box home improvement stores were beginning to look like any other mature business; slower growth and inroads by competitors had started to erode profit margins. Langone and other directors recognized that the founders had outgrown the business and that the company needed a new leader with experience improving efficiency and service. With this in mind, Langone suggested a candidate he knew from his

service on GE's board. Bob Nardelli, the former CEO of
GE Power Systems, was a talented executive with exactly
the kind of experience Home Depot needed. Cofounders
and directors Bernie Marcus and Arthur Blank quickly
realized the match between Nardelli's credentials and
the strategic challenges the company faced. Nardelli
proved to be the right choice. Despite flat sales and a
declining stock price due to the general economic slow-
down, the company is beginning once again to deliver on
earnings by taking cost out of the business. Had Langone
and the other directors failed to identify the specific
attributes required of the new CEO, they likely would
never have considered Nardelli—who had virtually no
retail experience—for the job.

Even when companies use search firms to find candidates, board members still must first identify the company's competitive challenges and industry context, as
well as the skills a replacement CEO will need. Doing so
will allow them to guide (rather than be guided by) the
recruiters. And it will ensure that recruiters look for a
specific set of skills and experiences, rather than simply
run through their Rolodexes of available executives.

SET REALISTIC PERFORMANCE
EXPECTATIONS

During the economic expansion of the 1980s and 1990s,
the investment community came to expect constant
improvement in earnings, and most executives and
boards were willing to prop up their stock prices by setting targets that pleased Wall Street. Though it's now
clear that this practice has created serious problems for
corporate America, the pressure from investors lingers.
New CEOs are often tempted to continue playing this

earnings game by promising unrealistic turnaround numbers, but that's precisely the wrong thing to do. Instead, the CEO needs to restart the clock by deflating unrealistic expectations, and the board needs to support that shift.

James Kilts was quick to reset expectations when he was appointed CEO at Gillette in January 2001. In his first meeting with analysts in June of that year, Kilts lambasted the unrealistic earnings forecasts set by Michael Hawley, his predecessor. Hawley had done everything possible to return Gillette to the 15% to 20% earnings growth it delivered during the 1990s. "Everything possible" included shortsighted practices such as channel stuffing—that is, shipping inventory ahead of consumption to meet overblown sales and earnings goals. Despite these practices (or perhaps because of them), the company was unable to deliver on the numbers, and the investment community lost confidence in Hawley.

Kilts believed that Gillette's managers were making decisions based on those looming earnings forecast, rather than on long-term strategic thinking. So, with the support of the board, he refused to provide the investment community with any financial targets at all, except for that of long-term sales growth of 3% to 5%. He told analysts that he and the board had decided not to give them guidance going forward. His refusal to play the game left the investment community perplexed; three analysts downgraded the stock, and only five out of 17 rated it a buy. Kilts stuck to his guns and focused his attention on the problems that had led to the earnings shortfalls. Analysts eventually noted that Gillette's product lines were rebuilding market share, and their confidence in the company's performance began to be restored. Recent earnings reports show that Gillette's strategy is beginning to pay off, and the stock has rebounded from its low.

The point isn't to starve the investment community of information—far from it. Though the wise board and CEO will back away from forecasts they can't meet, they'll also work extremely hard at communicating how they plan to address underlying competitive problems. After Jacques Nasser was dismissed from Ford, for example, William C. Ford, Jr., sent strong signals to investors. With advice and support from the board, he removed the executives perceived as responsible for Ford's problems. He also attempted to restore confidence in the company's finances by appointing former Wells Fargo Bank chairman and CEO Carl Reichardt as vice chairman, with the specific responsibility of overseeing Ford Financial. Then he announced a sweeping restructuring that trimmed production, rationalized car lines, reduced purchasing costs, and cut the labor force. These actions communicated the direction he and the board envisioned for the company more than any set of forecasted numbers could have done.

PROVIDE MORE STRATEGIC OVERSIGHT

And finally, good boards develop a deep understanding of the business and apply that understanding through active oversight of strategic performance. Once board members have appointed a new CEO, their job is far from over. They must resist the temptation to leave well enough alone for a while and remember that, since most replacement CEOs perform no better than their predecessors, they must be more vigilant than ever.

It's essential that boards provide strong strategic oversight following a dismissal because turnarounds aren't easy. They take subtlety, sophistication, and staying power. Consider General Motors. For nearly a decade under the leadership of Roger Smith, GM put profits ahead of sales—and watched its U.S. market share decline from 45% in 1980 to 36% in 1990. Eventually, the decline in market share eroded financial performance, and, despite the appointment of a new CEO, Robert Stempel, GM suffered losses in 1990 and 1991. The problems clearly went far beyond top leadership. GM offered too broad a range of product lines; the lines didn't share platforms or components; too many components were manufactured internally at higher costs; and the supply chain wasn't managed aggressively. Perhaps most important, central-office bureaucracy consistently stifled GM's ability to become a more innovative and efficient organization.

Following the back-to-back losses, Stempel, too, was dismissed, and the company finally got serious about turning itself around. The board appointed John F. Smith, Jr., who ultimately engineered GM's comeback. The board had to learn to be patient; the problems that had developed over a decade could not be solved overnight. Performance didn't improve much while Smith, with close oversight from the board, directed the much-needed overhaul: aggressively reducing costs through car platform rationalization, manufacturing consolidation, and outsourcing; spinning off the electrical components group, Delphi Automotive; selling aerospace business GM Hughes to Raytheon; and fundamentally restructuring the way the company conducted its business. Ultimately, GM improved its domestic and international operations and was rewarded with an increase in market share and a rebound in stock price. But that turnaround took almost a decade to accomplish—and it likely would never have happened at all if the board hadn't developed a sophisticated understanding of the complex, interconnected problems GM faced.

To ensure that they are providing proper oversight, board members should request from the CEO a strategic plan that identifies the options to consider, a timetable for a turnaround, most likely outcomes, and measures for evaluating whether the company is on track. Board members should closely question the assumptions underlying the strategic plan and how the proposed strategy alters the firm's risk factors and shapes its future direction. They should be willing to act if the new CEO does not improve the company's position in the marketplace. Despite the understandable desire to give the new CEO an extended honeymoon, members won't have fulfilled their primary fiduciary duty unless they formalize the responsibility to oversee strategy.

Target's board has figured out a way to fulfill its oversight function responsibly and constructively. The board formally reviews the CEO, and his or her progress on the strategic plan, every year. The chairman of the board encourages directors to make detailed inquiries, particularly when the company does not appear to be on track. The process is rigorous, but it's also very open; both the board and the executive team benefit from reviewing strategic assumptions together and debating strategic moves before they occur. The board's active oversight means that members are fulfilling their legal responsibility to the shareholders—and it also means they're giving the CEO far more feedback than most CEOs get. In the long run, this type of process is likely to foster stability at the helm since it encourages debate and questioning before a crisis emerges. The stronger the board, in other words, the less likely it is a company will have to fire its CEO in the first place.

The board and the CEO share responsibility for corporate performance, so it stands to reason that when a CEO fails, the board has failed as well. A good board will shoulder its share of the responsibility and commit to more diligent oversight in the future. Practically speaking, that means developing a better understanding of the business context; worrying less about pleasing the investment community and more about strategic fit when choosing a replacement; insisting on richer, fuller briefings from the new top-management team; and taking an active role in overseeing the CEO and the strategic performance of the company.

Originally published in December 2002
Reprint R0212E

Changing Leaders

The Board's Role in CEO Succession

JAY W. LORSCH AND RAKESH KHURANA

Executive Summary

THE SELECTION OF A CEO is one of the most important—and risky—events in the life of any company. Yet the way CEOs are chosen remains little discussed and little understood. The succession process has traditionally unfolded behind closed doors—some observers have even likened it to the election of a pope.

To shed light on what works and what doesn't in CEO succession, the authors lead a roundtable discussion with five distinguished corporate directors: Philip Caldwell, George D. Kennedy, G.G. Michelson, Henry Wendt, and Alfred M. Zeien. Collectively, the five directors have participated in dozens of successions, either as board members or as CEOs.

In a lively and frank exchange of views and experiences, the roundtable participants explore a broad range of questions: What can a company do to ensure a successful succession? How should management-development and succession processes be managed? How should the board work with the sitting chief executive during the process? What makes for a strong CEO candidate? When should outside candidates be considered? How much competition should be encouraged among potential CEO candidates? What role should executive search firms play? What role should former CEOs play after they are succeeded? Their conversation illuminates a corporate challenge that is as difficult as it is important.

T HE SELECTION OF A CEO is one of the most important decisions a board of directors makes. Not only does a chief executive have an enormous impact on the fortunes of a company, but the very process by which the executive is picked influences the way employees, investors, and other constituencies view the company and its leadership. Choosing a successor often places a strain on the entire management team, especially when the new executive comes from outside the company.

For all its obvious importance, the way CEOs are chosen remains little discussed and little understood. The succession process has traditionally unfolded behind closed doors—some observers have gone so far as to liken it to the election of a pope. In the past, such secrecy was taken for granted. Today it is not. As the visibility and power of CEOs have increased in recent years, so too have the stakes in CEO succession. A variety of parties, ranging from institutional investors to Wall Street analysts to business reporters, are now scrutinizing those responsible for CEO appointments and the way in which the appointments are made.

The demand for greater transparency in selecting chief executives comes at a time when the role that the board plays in succession is changing in fundamental ways. It used to be expected that CEOs would choose their own successors and that boards would simply rubber-stamp the choice. Today the relationship between the board and the CEO has become more complex. In an age of takeovers, mega-mergers, and global competition, boards rarely have the luxury of passivity. They need to be active players in shaping companies, and one place where they are taking a stronger hand is in overseeing the entire succession process. It is up to the board to ensure that the process is rigorous, careful, and—perhaps most important— defensible.

With these broader changes as a backdrop, we recently led a discussion on CEO succession with five distinguished corporate directors. Collectively, the five have served on dozens of boards and participated in a score of successions, and most of them have been or are currently CEOs themselves. Drawing on their deep experience, the directors discussed an array of topics: the hallmarks of a successful succession process, the relationship between the board and the sitting chief executive, the characteristics of a strong CEO candidate, the considerations in choosing an outsider, and the use of executive search firms. Their conversation sheds light on an obscure area of management, providing other directors and executives with models for action.

Jay Lorsch: A change in CEO is one of the most crucial events in the life of a company, and it is an event in which the board of directors plays a central role. Drawing on your experience as directors, how would you say that aboard could best ensure a smooth and successful succession?

Philip Caldwell: I would begin by laying out two assumptions. First, the best source of CEO candidates is the company itself. There are times when it will make sense to look outside, but in general you want successors to emerge from within the organization. Second, you want to have a choice of candidates—you don't want to narrow down to a single person too soon. With those two assumptions in mind, it seems to me that one of the board's most critical roles is to ensure the presence of an effective management development program for the whole enterprise. While the CEO will be the person managing the program, the board needs to play an active oversight role to ensure that the program is in place and that it's working effectively. The program should be formally reviewed by the board at least annually.

George Kennedy: Phil, what would you say are the key elements of a good management development program?

Caldwell: It needs to be stable—you don't want to be fiddling with it constantly. It needs to be viewed as a fundamental element of the administration of the business. It needs to be well understood by everyone throughout the organization. And it needs to be comprehensive, forming the basic personnel program for the whole company. It should not be designed to cover just the very top layer of management.

G.G. Michelson: I would recommend that it focus in depth on the top three tiers of managers. It should track their assignments, identify their development needs, and establish the career paths that will prepare them for higher responsibility. The board should be able to draw on information from the management development program to evaluate each manager in relation to the qualities that everyone has agreed are important for the successor CEO.

Henry Wendt: I agree about the importance of a strong management development program, but I don't think that management development and succession are necessarily synonymous. The board's supervision of the succession process should take place in the context of its broader responsibility for the organizational structure of the company, particularly the reporting relationships of senior executives. Those relationships, after all, define the routes traveled by the potential successors. At several companies on whose boards I've sat, I have insisted that the compensation committee's name be changed to the *organization* and compensation committee. That sends a very strong signal to everyone, including the CEO, that the board has the ultimate responsibility for the organizational structure as well as for the management development program and the choice of the successor. If the board doesn't keep a close eye on the structure, it will open the possibility that the CEO could manipulate the succession process.

Lorsch: Can you talk a little bit more about how the board actually evaluates the candidates coming up through the organization?

Kennedy: In addition to reviewing the information coming out of the development program, the board needs to have direct and regular contact with all the promising candidates. Some of the contact should be formal. For instance, you'll want to have the candidates make regular presentations at board meetings. But informal connections are also crucial. Board members need to take the time to get a feel for the personal chemistry of the candidates—to have casual conversations over dinner or lunch, for example. You have to have both formal and informal contacts to make sound judgments.

Wendt: Absolutely. You need both.

Michelson: I would add one ingredient. I think it's very important to try to establish situations in which you can see how the candidates relate to their peers. It's not enough just to look at how they act with the board or the CEO. I've seen talented executives who are very effective in their current jobs but who don't handle real authority well. It's hard to measure that capacity, but you can get a sense of it by seeing how individuals relate to their colleagues.

Caldwell: As companies have become more global, with managers all over the world, it has become harder to watch people in their everyday environment. But I agree that it's necessary. Both the CEO and the board should make it a high priority.

The Board and the CEO

Alfred Zeien: I think it's important that the board make sure the succession process begins about four years before the chief executive is expected to step down. It should require the CEO to clearly map out his or her plans for the process throughout that period. Four years gives you room to maneuver, and that's important. Let's say that a CEO looks out over the organization and sees that there's only one real candidate to succeed him. He's going to need to go out and bring new people into the to ranks of the company—to get the pool of potential successors up to three or four strong candidates. Getting those new people established and reviewing their performance takes time, so the board needs to insist that the process start early. And, to reiterate something that both Phil and Henry touched on, the board needs to prevent the CEO from steering the process toward one candidate. You've got to keep the options open.

Michelson: The board also has to make sure that the CEO feels comfortable changing his or her mind during that period. The candidate who looks best early in the process may not be the one who looks best later. It's often difficult for CEOs to admit they were mistaken, so it's incumbent upon the board to create a climate in which it becomes routine to reconsider opinions and points of view.

Kennedy: That requires good communication between the board and the CEO, which, as we all know, doesn't always exist. The board often fails to speak up, to challenge the CEO, either because it doesn't want to or because it's not organized to do so.

Wendt: Even when there is good communication between the board and the CEO, the chief executive may be too strong-minded to take guidance. He may listen, but he may not change. I can certainly think of a few examples of that.

Michelson: It is particularly apt to happen if the board is passive. Board members need to spend considerable time talking about the succession process, both with the CEO and among themselves.

Kennedy: G.G. raises a good point about the need for boards to talk without the CEO being present. That's not very common, but it's important. You need to have the opportunity to sit in executive session and talk frankly with your fellow board members about what's going well and what's not in the succession process, particularly concerning the chief executive's role. Those sessions should be a routine element of board meetings. Otherwise, the CEO may feel offended if he or she is suddenly asked to leave the room.

Wendt: I've been on boards where it was customary for the members to have discussions without the CEO, and those conversations were very helpful. We always designated one director to provide feedback to the CEO on any issues that came up in the session. Having a feedback mechanism makes the whole process less threatening to the CEO.

Kennedy: And more useful.

Wendt: Right.

Caldwell: But in creating some space between the CEO and the board, you need to be very careful that that space doesn't turn into a divide. The worst case is to have the relationship between the CEO and the board characterized by divisiveness or contention.

Kennedy: The board and the CEO have to remember that they have different roles. The CEO is the point person in the entire succession process—there's no question about that. But the CEO needs to understand that the board is going to make the ultimate decision on who the next CEO will be.

Zeien: I think in most cases the board would expect that the CEO would recommend a successor. At some point in the four-year process, he'll come forward and try to sell the board on the candidate he thinks is the best. For him to do that successfully, not only does he have to evaluate the candidates thoroughly and regularly, but he also has to keep sharing those evaluations with the board. He does not want to arrive at the end of the period and just say, "It's him" or "It's her." He has to have prepared the ground. And laying the groundwork is, of course, in his own best interest; otherwise, he's going to have a difficult time convincing the board that his choice is the right choice.

Wendt: I was once involved in a situation where that kind of groundwork was lacking. The CEO strongly recommended a candidate, but the board was deeply divided. About one-third of the directors supported the choice, another third were violently opposed, and the rest were on the fence. It became not just a succession problem but a problem of holding the board together and keeping the whole governance of the corporation intact.

Lorsch: How did it turn out?

Wendt: In the end, it worked out reasonably well, but it was a very threatening episode—the most dramatic internal crisis I've seen. I happened to be the chairman of the compensation committee, so I remember it distinctly. We had about a year before the CEO stepped down, and in the course of that year, the board met in at least ten serious executive sessions. It took a lot of discussion and debate, but the board held together, and we ended up choosing a candidate other than the CEO's. And, I'm happy to say, it was the right choice. I remain convinced that the CEO's choice would have been a disaster.

Avoiding a Horse Race

Rakesh Khurana: We've talked about the importance of identifying several candidates—three or four was the number Al mentioned, I think. Do you want to encourage competition among that group, or do you want to minimize the competitiveness?

Michelson: There will inevitably be competition, but too much is dangerous. If you turn it into an overt horse race, you'll lose a great deal of talent once the ultimate decision is made. A number of years ago, I witnessed a succession process that turned into a horse race—a long, public horse race—and the company ended up losing a lot of very good people. The company chose the right person in the end, but the process was much more painful than it needed to be. In a succession situation, you're probably going to lose good people whatever you do, but you'll guarantee a mass exodus if you make the competition too open.

Kennedy: Turning it into a public competition is unfair and unproductive.

Lorsch: So far we've been talking about what I'll term a "natural transition," where the departure of the existing CEO is planned well in advance. Sometimes, though, chief executives leave unexpectedly—they may not be performing well, for instance, or they may get ill. They may decide that they can get a better job someplace else. What does the board do under those circumstances? How would the process change?

Michelson: In emergencies, good management development and succession processes become all the more valuable. If you have the mechanisms in place to monitor in-depth the performance of the next natural group of successors, you'll be well equipped to decide who ought to step in or to know that no one's yet ready for the post.

Kennedy: If no one is ready, you need to be prepared to bring in a caretaker—a person who takes charge for a period of time but who is not necessarily the succeeding CEO.

Michelson: Often, it will be an executive who's deeply experienced but is too advanced in age to act as chief executive for the long term.

Caldwell: Bringing in an interim CEO is sometimes necessary, but it's not ideal in my view. You should always try to have someone in the organization who could take over effectively as chief executive at a moment's notice. If at times you have to bring outsiders in to add depth to the top management team, so be it. It's best to have someone capable in the wings.

Zeien: On a practical note, you can do some things to prepare for such emergencies. I work on two boards where the CEO is required to leave with the head of the personnel committee a letter detailing what should happen if the CEO suddenly gets hit by a trolley car.

Michelson: When I chaired the compensation or management-development committees in a variety of companies, I annually asked the CEOs to designate someone who in their judgment should take over in an emergency. I did it every year because the CEO's view can change. And I always asked the committee and the board if they wanted me to open the envelope. Sometimes they did, and sometimes they didn't.

The Makings of a CEO

Khurana: Most candidates for the CEO post will be heads of business units or other divisions. What does it take to move up from such a position to CEO? What qualities do you look for?

Michelson: The qualities you look for in a CEO are different from those you look for in the leader of an individual business. A CEO has to have a strategic vision for the company. That's a hard thing to judge because business managers are rarely required to have a strategic view of the broader company.

Wendt: And a CEO has to be able to represent the company to outside constituencies, which is not something that business heads usually have to do.

Zeien: What's most difficult to gauge is how an individual will act once he or she is at the very top of the organization. As people rise through the ranks, it's fairly easy to track their accomplishments, to see how well they've worked with other people and how well they've formulated plans for their particular units, but those kinds of measures tell you little about how someone will respond to being in charge. I've seen very capable people who all through their careers have depended on the encouragement they receive from their bosses. Once they get into the corner office, there's suddenly no one there to pat them on the back. It's an entirely different kind of job.

Kennedy: I couldn't agree more. There's a mystery component that is really difficult to evaluate. All of a sudden, you've got a chauffeur and a limousine, you have an expense account that hardly anybody asks about, and you've got all kinds of temptations to let power go to your head. Whether or not a person will be staunch and sturdy enough to stand up to the temptations is a tremendous challenge for the board to judge.

Wendt: The CEO is often required to make very lonely decisions—there's a solitary aspect to the job—but the management development process tends to place a strong emphasis on team play. A great team player will not necessarily make a great CEO.

Lorsch: If you're in a large, international company, I suppose you can gain a sense of how a person would

*respond to the top position by having him or her run a
big unit that's distant from headquarters.*

Michelson: That can be helpful, but it's not foolproof.
I've been in a situation where the CEO recommended a
successor who had excelled at heading a big, distant
business, and the board was unanimous in endorsing the
choice. Yet when the guy assumed the top job, he didn't
know how to handle the authority. He turned out to be
overly autocratic, and we hadn't been able to foresee that.

Zeien: I've found that one way to gain insight into
that mystery component is to pay close attention to how
well the individual listens. When others are presenting
information or expressing their points of view, is the
person really listening to what they have to say, or is he
just formulating his reply? Many of the problems that
otherwise-talented people have when they become chief
executives can be traced to their inability to listen.

Kennedy: Another thing that you have to look at is
the candidate's personal stability, and that requires some
knowledge of his or her family life and other activities
outside the corporation. The better you know the person's sense of ethics and ability to put up with pressure,
the better you can judge whether or not the person is
going to be swayed by the power of the CEO office.

Choosing an Outsider

*Khurana: We've been focusing so far on successors who
come from within the organization. But although most
companies continue to pick insiders, studies indicate
that about a third of new CEOs are now brought in from
outside. What underlies this trend? And what are the
signs that an outsider might be the best choice for an
organization?*

Caldwell: It used to be that a company was in one kind of business and stayed in it. Today, companies are much more likely to shift between businesses. We see this dynamic at work in many of the mergers and acquisitions that have become so commonplace. A manufacturer may buy a financial service provider; all of a sudden, it's in a different business, and running that business requires a different set of skills. The internal CEO candidates may have been appropriate for the old company, but they may not be right for the new company. A similar thing can happen when an organization expands into new international markets, which also is happening more and more these days.

Wendt: Even beyond acquisitions and globalization, the overall pace of change in business is accelerating, which puts pressure on companies to reinvent themselves. It can be very hard for someone within a company to lead such radical change. It may take an outsider to do the job.

Michelson: Another force at work is the increasing mobility of managers. You can't count on people to be lifers anymore. That means you're going to have more turnover in the executive ranks, and as a result there will be a smaller pool of natural internal successors.

Kennedy: For all those reasons, it's becoming more politically correct to go outside. It used to be a no-no.

Zeien: In my view, though, it's still a sign of failure. If you've established a good succession process, extending over a full four years, you should have a worthy group of successors in place.

Michelson: I agree. I'm a director of one company that will be facing a critical succession in a few years, and we have a strong set of candidates. As a director, I would be very embarrassed if we didn't have that kind of talent in place. I'd regard myself as having failed in my responsibility.

Wendt: But I'd go back to my point about the pace of change in business today. Even if you've done a good job grooming internal candidates, changes in the competitive landscape, in technological platforms, in the customer base—any or all of these—can sometimes create such profound dislocations that you have to rethink your criteria for a CEO. In those instances, you may have no choice but to go outside. The future of the company may bear little resemblance to its past or its present.

Michelson: But knowing such changes can happen, shouldn't you have been taking them into account throughout the succession process? Shouldn't the ability to cope with such challenges have been part of the criteria you've been using to evaluate candidates?

Wendt: That would be the ideal, of course. But in reality not all management development programs fulfill the ideal. There have been some great, great companies— IBM is a wonderful example—that didn't keep step with the pace of change. They've had to look outside their walls for their new leaders—and at least in IBM's case— it's worked out very well.

Khurana: When you do go with an outsider, what is the effect on internal executives, particularly those who had been candidates for the top spot? When a company initiates a succession process, isn't it making an implicit promise to its top people that the next CEO will be one of them?

Michelson: When you bring in an outsider, most of your best people will head for the exits.

Wendt: That's a real risk. It's much better to introduce outside talent into the executive pool before the CEO departs than to suddenly name an outsider as the chief executive.

Michelson: Now we're in full agreement, Henry. I would even say you should make it a formal operating policy to regularly seed the management team with outsiders. That helps prevent a company from becoming inbred, and it helps avoid the kind of abrupt cultural revolution you set off when you hire an external chief executive.

The Role of the Executive Search Firm

Khurana: The question of outside candidates naturally brings us to the question of how executive search firms should or should not be used in the succession process. How do you see the role of a search firm?

Kennedy: You ought to start with the understanding that you are better off if you don't need one. To expect an executive search firm to do the board's job is a miscalculation.

Michelson: But if you do need to use one, I've found that they're more helpful in the role of verifying qualifications and references than in identifying wonderful talent. A board's search committee can usually identify more good candidates than an executive search firm.

Kennedy: I have to say, though, that there are people in search firms who can open the door to candidates that otherwise would be likely to turn you down. There may be an executive out there who has been approached 35 times by different companies in the last year and has turned them all down, but the right search firm can sometimes get through and make the connection.

Wendt: A search firm can also help the board evaluate executive quality throughout the industry. As outside directors, most of us don't come from the industry that the company competes in. Working with a search firm can help us develop benchmarks of executive quality in the industry. That's often very useful.

Zeien: I've found that a search firm is only as good as the specification it receives from the board. We talked earlier about how difficult it is to judge a person's ability to assume the top spot in a company. Making that judgment become seven more difficult when you're pulling someone in from outside. Most companies have distinct cultures—some almost look more like cults than cultures—and it's extremely hard to gauge how an outsider will fit in. The board has to develop a clear, detailed spec for the position—that's a role that it cannot offload to the search consultant. The spec should guide the search and should form the basis for the board's ultimate decision. A good spec won't guarantee success, but it will certainly improve the odds.

Managing the Changeover

Khurana: It can be tough for successful CEOs to give up their posts. Is there a danger that a CEO can end up staying on too long? And how can a board help prevent such a situation?

Kennedy: I think your question again underscores the importance of establishing a clear, lengthy process for the succession—a four-year process, as Al suggested. That gives the sitting chief executive time to begin the transition to a new life after the company, which can indeed be a highly traumatic change. By establishing a definite end point well in the future, you make sure that the CEO won't suddenly get cold feet and start postponing his or her departure. Once the train gets started down the track, it becomes very difficult for the CEO to stop it.

Michelson: Establishing a mandatory retirement age can also help provide a structure that ensures a smooth, timely transition. I'm not saying it's right for every company and every board, but it's a practice that has served a number of companies well.

Wendt: It's also useful to have an annual meeting between the outside directors and the CEO where the topic of retirement is discussed. You lay out the CEO's timetable, the board's timetable, and you review the succession candidates. By having that discussion every year, you help the process move forward to its natural conclusion on time.

Michelson: The board should also emphasize to the CEO that one of the most important measures of his success is how well he handles the succession—not just by preparing the next generation of leaders but by actually moving aside to let them take over. Underscoring that point can help a CEO realize the seriousness of the role he plays in succession.

Zeien: It's worth noting that one of the great strengths of the public corporation—the American-style public corporation—is its formalized succession process and the expectation that top executives will move on when they're still at the height of their capabilities. You don't find that in private companies, where founders often never retire, and you don't find it in most universities or hospitals or governmental bodies. The U.S. public corporation is unique in its assumption of a limited tenure for its chief executive, and I think that is a very positive thing.

Lorsch: I think that brings us around to our last question. Should a retired CEO continue to play a role in the company?

Michelson: While acknowledging that Phil Caldwell is an exception, I have to say that I believe in sudden death.

Wendt: I second that. The answer, in today's world, is no.

Michelson: In fact, I would say your successor is much more likely to come and ask your advice or get your opinion if you're not sitting on the board, if you've severed your formal connection to the company.

Kennedy: I once made the mistake of staying on the board after retiring as CEO, and I wouldn't do it again. An issue would come up for a decision, and the other board members would look to me as the former CEO and then look to the new CEO. The mere fact that they looked to see my expression—to try to gauge my feelings—was a terrible disservice to the new CEO.

Wendt: In two instances, I served as chief executive when the former CEOs were on the board, and it made things very uncomfortable. It's hard to propose changes without that being interpreted as a personal criticism of your predecessor. It's a terrible handicap.

Zeien: I'm not sure I'd say it never makes sense for the CEO to remain on the board. In some companies—Procter & Gamble, for instance—it's a tradition, and it seems to work for them. But one thing that I think is almost always a mistake is having the CEO move into a non-executive chairmanship. That doesn't work.

Kennedy: My feeling is that upon retirement the CEO becomes the exclusive problem of his or her spouse.

Lorsch: George, I think we'll let that stand as the last word. On behalf of Rakesh and myself, I want to thank you all for spending time with us today. You've helped illuminate a corporate challenge that is as difficult as it is important. Thanks to all of you very much.

The Participants

Philip Caldwell succeeded Henry Ford II as CEO of Ford Motor Company in 1979 and as chairman in 1980. He retired in 1985, continuing to serve as a member of the board until 1990. From 1985 to 1998, he was senior managing director of Lehman Brothers. Currently, he is a director of the Mexico Fund, Mettler-Toledo, Zurich Holding Company of America, American Guarantee & Liability Insurance Company, Russell Reynolds Associates, and Waters Corporation. He is a former director of the Chase Manhattan Corporation, Castech Aluminum Group, Digital Equipment, Federated Department Stores, and the Kellogg Company, among other organizations.

George D. Kennedy is the former chairman and CEO of International Minerals and Chemical Corporation and of the Mallinckrodt Group. He also served as president of Brown Company and of Nationwide Papers. He is a director of Kemper Insurance Companies, Scotsman Industries, American National Can Company, and HealthShare Technology. He is a managing partner of Berkshire Capital Investors and a former director of Illinois Tool Works, Stone Container Corporation, and the Brunswick Corporation.

G.G. Michelson held numerous executive positions during her long career with R.H. Macy & Company and served on its board of directors. She retired from the company as senior vice president for external affairs in 1992. She is a director of the General Electric Company, president of the board of overseers of TIAA-CREF, and chairperson emerita of the board of trustees of Columbia University. She is a former director of many companies, including the Rand Corporation, the Irving Bank Corporation, Harper & Row Publishers, the Quaker Oats Company, Federated Department Stores, the Stanley Works, the Chubb Corporation, and the Goodyear Tire and Rubber Company.

Henry Wendt retired as chairman of Smith-Kline Beecham in 1994 after a four-decade career in the pharmaceutical, health care, and services industries. He is currently chairman of Global Health Care Partners and serves on the board of directors of Allergan, Atlantic Richfield Company, Computerized Medical Systems, the Egypt Investment Company, West Marine Products, and Wilson Greatbatch. He is the author of *Global Embrace* (Harper Business, 1993).

Alfred M. Zeien recently retired as chairman and CEO of the Gillette Company. He was elected to those positions in 1991, after serving in a variety of international executive posts since joining the company in 1968. He continues to serve on Gillette's board, and he is also a director of BankBoston Corporation, Polaroid Corporation, the Massachusetts Mutual Life Insurance Company, and Raytheon Company. He also serves as a trustee or director of a number of nonprofit and educational institutions.

Originally published in May 1999
Reprint 99308

Seven Surprises for New CEOs

MICHAEL E. PORTER, JAY W. LORSCH,
AND NITIN NOHRIA

Executive Summary

AS A NEWLY MINTED CEO, you may think you
finally have the power to set strategy, the authority
to make things happen, and full access to the finer
points of your business. But if you expect the job to
be as simple as that, you're in for an awakening.
Even though you bear full responsibility for your
company's well-being, you are a few steps
removed from many of the factors that drive results.
You have more power than anybody else in the
corporation, but you need to use it with extreme
caution.

In their workshops for new CEOs, held at
Harvard Business School in Boston, the authors
have discovered that nothing—not even running a
large business within the company—fully prepares

a person to be the chief executive. The seven most common surprises are:

- You can't run the company.
- Giving orders is very costly.
- It is hard to know what is really going on.
- You are always sending a message.
- You are not the boss.
- Pleasing shareholders is not the goal.
- You are still only human.

These surprises carry some important and subtle lessons. First, you must learn to manage organizational context rather than focus on daily operations. Second, you must recognize that your position does not confer the right to lead, nor does it guarantee the loyalty of the organization. Finally, you must remember that you are subject to a host of limitations, even though others might treat you as omnipotent. How well and how quickly you understand, accept, and confront the seven surprises will have a lot to do with your success or failure as a CEO.

Bearing full responsibility for a company's success or failure, but being unable to control most of what will determine it. Having more authority than anyone else in the organization, but being unable to wield it without unhappy consequences. Sound like a tough job? It is—ask a CEO. Surprised by the description? So are CEOs who are new to the role. Just when an executive feels he has reached the pinnacle of his career, capturing the coveted goal for which he has so long been striving, he begins to realize that the CEO's job is different and more complicated than he imagined.

Some of the surprises for new CEOs arise from time and knowledge limitations—there is so much to do in complex new areas, with imperfect information and never enough time. Others stem from unexpected and unfamiliar new roles and altered professional relationships. Still others crop up because of the paradox that the more power you have, the harder it is to use. While several of the challenges may appear familiar, we have discovered that nothing in a leader's background, even running a large business within his company, fully prepares him to be CEO.

Through our work with new chief executives of major companies, we have found seven surprises to be the most common. (See the sidebar "Learning the Ropes.") How well and how quickly new CEOs understand, accept, and confront them will have a lot to do with the executives' eventual success or failure. The seven surprises highlight realities about the nature of leadership that are important not just for CEOs but for executives at any level and in any size organization.

Surprise One: You Can't Run the Company

Before becoming CEO, most executives are responsible for a major business or have been COO. They are skilled at running businesses and relish the opportunity to run an entire organization. As new CEOs discover pretty quickly, however, running the business is but a small part of the job. On the second day of our New CEO Workshop at Harvard Business School, we go around the room and ask

participants to describe what the job feels like to them.
At a recent session, the CEO of a large midwestern
manufacturer—an executive whose practiced, confident
air bespoke decades of experience—revealed just how
unsure he felt as he took his first steps on this new ground:

*Imagine serving the same company for 37 years. It is
the only employer you have ever known, and this fact
intensifies the tremendous loyalty you feel for the firm
and the camaraderie you share with your colleagues.
Your appointment to CEO was one of the proudest
moments of your life. You have been training to run
the business for your whole career, you think, and you
are really looking forward to doing so.*

*Now fast-forward a few months. Your calendar is
booked solid with analyst meetings, business media
interviews (which take ages to prepare for, since you
never know where the shots will come from), and sessions in Washington (where you will attempt to explain
to politicians the crucial and intricate details of your
industry). You have also recently been elected to an
outside directorship or two, and the charities that you
have long supported are more eager than ever for you
to join their boards and raise funds on their behalf. No
one will accept a substitute—it has to be you.*

*Not only do you have external pressures tugging you
away from day-to-day business operations; the volume
of internal demands is enormous. Before you became
CEO, you prided yourself on visiting every unit in your
region, you got to know the employees, you spoke
directly with customers—you had your hands right on
the pulse of the business. Since you have become CEO,
you have not been able to do any of these things even*

*for your old region—never mind the rest. You cannot
shake the feeling that you have lost touch with the day-
to-day workings of your company. To make matters
worse, the unavoidable gaps in your own expertise
loom larger than ever.*

This type of response is typical; a new CEO's comfort
and familiarity with internal operations quickly recede
as demands on the executive mount. The sheer volume
and intensity of external demands take many by surprise.
Almost every new CEO struggles to manage the time
drain of attending to shareholders, analysts, board members, industry groups, politicians, and other constituencies. CEOs hired from outside struggle to learn how their
new company operates, but those promoted from within
work equally hard to separate themselves from operations and learn the terrain of their outside constituencies. Some have told us quite frankly that they feel a
sense of loss because they're no longer as close to the
business as they once were. One participant in the New
CEO Workshop who had come up through the ranks at
his company told us that he felt as if he were starting all
over again—he had to learn new management tools and
build new relationships while reframing old ones. Workshop participants complete a forced-rank survey that
asks how prepared they feel for their new responsibilities
on a number of dimensions, such as dealing with the
stock market, working with their board of directors,
operating at the center of public scrutiny, building a
senior management team, or being the company's chief
spokesperson. It is clear from their responses that CEOs
are apprehensive about, as one put it, managing the dual
roles of Mr. Inside and Mr. Outside.

As the CEO learns how demanding it is to attend to the company's outside constituencies, he also discovers, often to his shock, that he has to let go of a lot of responsibility—not just for operating the company but even for knowing what's going on in it. The CEO can't monitor everyone. It's simply not possible for any one person to oversee every facet of a large company, even if he were willing to put in a 100-hour week. The new CEO may expect this to be true as he begins, but it still feels strange not to know what subordinates are up to, and many executives experience the change as a loss of control. One workshop participant recalled that he was stunned by the realization that he would have to rely on others in areas like operations, where he had previously thrived, and would have to master aspects of the company such as investor relations and regulatory affairs, where he had little experience. To be sure, the new CEO has the final say in hiring and firing, promotions, and compensation, but many of those decisions are, by necessity, in the hands of people closer to operations. Indeed, CEOs often end up knowing less about the operational details of their companies than they did in their previous positions.

While the CEO is responsible for the successful operation of the enterprise, then, he can no longer be personally involved in all the decisions needed to run a large, complex organization. The CEO's greatest influence shifts from direct to indirect means—articulating and communicating a clear, easily understood strategy; institutionalizing rigorous structures and processes to guide, inform, and reward; and setting values and tone. Equally important is selecting and managing the right senior management team to share the burden of running the company.

Surprise Two: Giving Orders Is Very Costly

The CEO is undoubtedly the most powerful person in any organization. Yet any CEO who tries to use this power to unilaterally issue orders or summarily reject proposals that have come up through the organization will pay a stiff price. Giving orders can trigger resentment and defensiveness in colleagues and subordinates. Second-guessing a senior manager can demoralize and demotivate not only that person but others around him, while eroding his authority and confidence. What's more, the need to overrule a proposal indicates that the strategic planning and other processes in place may be either inappropriate or insufficient. No proposal should reach the CEO for final approval unless he can ratify it with enthusiasm. Before then, everyone involved with the matter should have raised and resolved any potential deal breakers, bringing the CEO into the discussion only at strategically significant moments to obtain feedback and support. Ironically, by exercising his power to give orders, the CEO actually reduces his real power, saps his energy and his organization's, and slows down progress.

When CEOs wield direct power, they must do so very selectively and deliberately—and never without a broader plan of action in mind. Usually, power is best used indirectly, through the disciplined processes mentioned above (articulating strategy and so on). Together with tone and style, such processes enable the CEO to make effective decisions consistent with where he wants the company to go.

One of our new CEOs learned this the hard way. Soon after he became CEO, he was asked to approve a marketing campaign for the launch of a new product. The campaign was the result of more than a year's work by a division manager and his team. They had developed advertising, prepared promotional materials, crafted a sales and distribution plan, and assigned responsibilities for different parts of the plan. All that was needed was the new CEO's approval, which the executives assumed was largely a formality.

The CEO saw it differently. He felt that the company's advertising had become stale and that a makeover should start right away—and this would most likely mean hiring a new agency. He put the marketing campaign on hold until a new advertising plan could be developed—a decision that he hoped would send a strong signal about the changes he meant to introduce. Little did he realize that he had sent several other powerful signals as well.

Word of his order spread like wildfire. The CEO's calendar was soon filled with meetings with executives seeking approval of their plans. Some came to obtain consent for new capital expenditures, others for personnel decisions, and others on matters as mundane as whether to host a client conference. They had lost confidence that they understood the CEO's expectations, so they wanted to check with him before proceeding on anything. His calendar became a bottleneck, and organizational decision making virtually ground to a halt.

For a while, the CEO was oblivious to the high cost of his intrusive approach. As an outsider new to the company, he felt good about being part of all these conversations. He was now at the center of all the action. He viewed each meeting as an opportunity to communicate the new direction in which he hoped to take the company. But he began to recognize the impact of his actions when the division manager he had overruled came forward a month later with the news that he had decided to

accept a job at another company. This came as a shock
to the CEO, who, despite nixing the ad campaign, had
been quite impressed with the other elements of the
marketing program and the thoroughness with which
they had been planned. What he had failed to understand was that he had undermined the manager's self-
confidence as well as his authority with his subordinates
and peers. As hard as the CEO tried to persuade him to
reconsider and stay, the manager felt so demoralized
that he was determined to leave.

Chastened, the CEO called a meeting of all his top
managers the next week. He reassured them that they
enjoyed his full confidence and that he had no intention
of undermining their authority as he had done with the
departing division manager. He candidly admitted that
he might have been too precipitous in halting the marketing campaign, especially since he had not yet fully
communicated his new strategy for the company. He
identified the areas in which he wanted to make strategic
changes, emphasizing that all this was a work in
progress, to be completed with everyone's help. He clari-
fied the issues on which he wanted to be consulted and
those on which he would fully trust his managers. He
created a task force to review some of the company's key
management processes—planning, budgeting, performance evaluation, new product rollout, development of
marketing campaigns, and recruitment of key employees—
to ensure that there would be opportunities for early
CEO input. Finally, he spent the next year working hard
to make sure that his vision and agenda were clear to all
employees, especially his senior management team. (We
know this because he stayed in touch with us after the
workshop, as many participants do.)

This CEO concluded, and we would agree, that it is
rarely a good idea to unilaterally overrule a thoughtful

decision that has cleared several other organizational hurdles. Indeed, a key indicator the CEO subsequently used to judge the health of the company's management processes was how enthusiastically he could approve the decisions that came his way. The need to overrule something is a sure sign of a broader organizational failure. Or, as hard as this is to admit, it may reflect the CEO's own failure to clearly communicate his strategy and operating principles. There are certainly some circumstances in which the harm done by moving forward with a major strategic decision that the CEO considers a serious mistake—a large acquisition, say—is greater than the harm done by issuing orders. But, as this CEO himself eventually acknowledged, the ad makeover could have waited.

A new CEO may need to put a stake in the ground to show that he's in charge and to let the organization know what he stands for. Giving a direct order (and especially undoing someone's work) is rarely the best way to do this, however. Instead, a CEO should look for ways to include senior managers and to promote agreement about decision-making criteria. At an off-site meeting, for example, the CEO can reveal his priorities and concerns by setting the agenda while giving his team a chance to participate and buy in. A new CEO must be willing to share power and trust others to make important decisions. The most powerful CEO is the one who expands the power of those around him.

Surprise Three: It Is Hard to Know What Is Really Going On

Even when CEOs understand that they cannot oversee every aspect of their companies, they nevertheless

assume—wrongly—that they will be able to learn everything they need to know. Certainly, CEOs are flooded
with information, but reliable information is surprisingly
scarce. All information coming to the top is filtered,
sometimes with good intentions, sometimes with not
such good intentions. Receiving solid information
becomes even more difficult because immediately upon
appointment, the CEO's relationships change. Former
peers and subordinates who used to constitute an informal channel—those who could read between the lines
and who really knew what was happening at the ground
level—go on their guard. Even those the CEO was closest
to are wary of delivering bad news. Further, because the
CEO can have so much impact on anyone's career, each
individual's agenda colors the information the CEO
receives.

Look at the experience of one workshop participant,
whose organization was an equal partner in a poorly performing joint venture. As revenues failed to materialize
and costs continued to rise, the CEO tried to better
understand the lackluster performance by holding several reviews with key managers involved in the venture.
Their explanations for the unimpressive results were not
surprising: The managers placed the blame squarely on
the JV partner. When it became clear to the CEO that he
would not find out what was really going on simply by
asking his own team for information, he approached
senior managers from the other company—ones who, as
it happened, were not directly involved in the JV's operations. Their understanding of the situation was different
from what the CEO's own people had been telling him,
and the partner's managers offered many constructive
observations on the JV's operations. In the end, the CEO
recognized that the root cause of the problems was a

lack of clarity—on both sides of the partnership—about the JV's objectives. His company eventually bought its way out of the venture, at a loss.

Looking back, the CEO did not feel that his team hid information with malicious intent. For one thing, he realized, his people had a natural instinct to protect themselves, especially in front of their leader. Others who knew how serious the problems were perhaps refrained from speaking up because they were concerned that the CEO would shoot the messenger. Also, it was inherently difficult for operating management to recognize the problem, which lay not in operational details but in the unclear and clashing goals with which the joint venture was established. For the CEO, the biggest surprise was having to seek external feedback to better assess what was really going on within his organization, because a clear picture was so hard to get from his own people.

It is a delicate challenge for a CEO to find reliable sources of information without undermining key reports, who might feel that the CEO is going around them. Many workshop participants recounted their efforts to engage in periodic face-to-face conversations with people at different levels and in various parts of the company. One CEO, for example, invited a group of ten to 12 employees to have lunch with him weekly. Employees volunteered to participate, and the group included people from all levels and divisions; managers were not allowed to attend with their direct reports. While the CEO recognized that not everyone in these lunches would speak frankly, he found that an informal setting reduced barriers to communication and provided an opportunity to hear the ideas and opinions of a cross section of employees. Other CEOs described using field visits and town-hall-type forums to pickup relatively unfiltered information.

Several new CEOs stressed the importance of continuing to seek information from deep within the organization—from employees closest to the front line—even though that approach might not sit well with managers in the middle. A CEO of a high-technology firm, for example, went several levels down to determine the status of technical projects by asking those directly involved how the work was progressing. He didn't tell the senior people overseeing the projects that he was taking these surprise "temperature checks." Another CEO took it as a warning sign if senior executives tried to discourage him from speaking directly to their subordinates. He underscored, however, that this sort of contact worked only if it was maintained regularly, so that it was not considered a big event—and if the people who spoke to the CEO felt confident that their candor would not come back to haunt them.

Many CEOs in the workshop find that unbiased information is available from external channels—for instance, through contact with customers, conversations with other CEOs, and affiliations with industry associations. Almost every workshop participant allocated time for such external discussions through a systematic process. Several CEOs also pointed to productive relationships they had with independent advisers who could tell the unabashed truth and had license to criticize the CEO's thinking.

Surprise Four: You Are Always Sending a Message

The typical new CEO knows that his actions will be noticed by those in his company. What he does not generally realize is the extent to which his every move—both inside and outside the organization—will be scrutinized and interpreted. His words and deeds, however small or off-the-cuff, are instantly spread and amplified, and sometimes drastically misinterpreted. (Remember the CEO who pulled the marketing campaign.) Even personal choices are subject to scrutiny. One CEO in our workshop joked that he had to choose the type of car he drove very carefully because the company parking lot would soon be full of the same model.

The first big message is in the CEO's appointment itself. People develop assumptions and expectations based on the CEO's background and previous experiences. This initial profile immediately takes on great significance. One CEO, the first American to take the helm of his major British company, reflected in our workshop that many constituencies expected the "barbaric American" to try to change the firm's centuries-old traditions and culture. A CEO with a legal background recounted how the markets reacted negatively to his appointment, on the assumption that the only reason to make a lawyer CEO was that the company was facing deeper asbestos-litigation problems than previously acknowledged. These sorts of messages are sent before the new CEO even does anything.

Once in the job, the new CEO can no longer afford to have speculative discussions with employees, employees, because any half-baked idea he puts forth runs the risk of being latched onto as a good one. The CEO's microphone is always on, and his message can become distorted. Even an innocent question may be interpreted as a loss of confidence. The aura attached to the executive's words is illustrated in a story we heard from one CEO, who found, to his surprise, that too many people were invoking his name—hoping that simply starting a sentence with "Frank says. . ." would ensure action, even

though, in most cases, Frank hadn't said anything of
the sort.

And so new CEOs need to learn quickly what signals
they are sending. They can then minimize inadvertent
messages and maximize the impact of the messages they
want to send, once they understand the multiplier effect
of their words and actions. Consider, for example, the
experience of one new CEO, whose organization is based
in the southeastern United States. The company had
avoided racially related class action lawsuits, even
though other companies in the region had not. It had
clear standards covering employee behavior, including a
rule forbidding the display of the Confederate flag. When
the local press revealed that one member of the executive team had publicly advocated that the company
display the flag, the CEO immediately had that person
terminated. As the CEO described it, he did this to signal
that behavior inconsistent with company policy would
not be tolerated at any level in the organization. No one
had to guess the CEO's views on this topic—he sent a
clear message.

To take another example, a new CEO of a transportation company wanted to signal the importance of
customer and employee safety. While on a site visit, he
noticed that a fire switch was disconnected on one rail
car, so he shut down all trains in the system until every
switch could be checked. He also launched an investigation into why the switch was disconnected, to prevent
a reoccurrence. Although there were redundant systems
in place, the CEO wanted his actions to send a message—
both internally and externally—that nothing short of
perfect safety compliance would be acceptable. He also
hoped that employees would in turn feel empowered to
do whatever was necessary to ensure safety.

A CEO's signals, already subject to misinterpretation, are further complicated by the fact that different con- stituencies will respond to the same news in different ways. It is particularly challenging when signals are sent to both internal and external groups. While Wall Street might delight in hearing a plan for a struggling unit's spin-off, for instance, employees may be shattered. The task of managing outside and inside constituencies, while keeping the message truthful and consistent to both, is never easy. The important lesson for new CEOs is to consider carefully how their actions and the way these are communicated will be interpreted by different audi- ences. An executive may be unable to avoid some nega- tive impact on one group or another, but by thoughtfully framing his message, he can minimize the damage.

Finally, to the extent possible, CEOs must strive for consistency in their messages. A simple, clear message, repeated often and illustrated with memorable stories, is the best way for a new CEO to master the communica- tion challenges of the job.

Surprise Five: You Are Not the Boss

Many new CEOs initially assume that they have finally reached a position where they have ultimate authority. They soon learn that the situation is much more compli- cated than that. Although the CEO may sit at the top of the management hierarchy, he still reports to the board of directors. The board hired him and can also fire him; it has the power to evaluate his performance, set his com- pensation, overturn his strategy, and make other major decisions. CEOs must attend to this relationship more today than ever before as new laws and regulations, court decisions, and shareholder activism have empowered and emboldened boards. As one new CEO told us, "We no longer have a clear picture of how to work with the board." Even if the relationship isn't contentious, it's become a bigger drain on the CEO's time and energy.

Just when new CEOs think they can finally stop managing upward, the need to do so grows in complexity. Instead of reporting to a single boss, the new CEO has ten or 12 bosses, one of whom is often a "lead director," who, by virtue of that position, is meant to balance the CEO's authority. And although the board is likely to comprise experienced and capable people, many members will have limited knowledge of the company's industry. This means the CEO (along with the management team) has to educate the board about what is happening in the company and the industry. While the CEO may have problems in getting information, the worst thing for his relationship with the board is for the directors to feel uninformed or surprised. Because board members have many demands on their time, information must be transmitted to them in a way that is easy to understand.

Moreover, most board members may have had little previous contact with the new CEO. Even if he was promoted from within and was previously on the board, their interaction with him was probably infrequent and brief. He has to spend time letting members get to know him and develop confidence in his ability and judgment. Should the new CEO's predecessor remain involved, in the chairman's seat or on the board, the challenge becomes even greater. The former CEO brings board relationships and a legacy of decisions that the new CEO may wish to reconsider. All of this creates awkwardness in the boardroom and makes it difficult for the successor to work with the board. In our experience, it is almost always a bad idea for a predecessor to remain on the board.

For one new CEO, the first few weeks in office were a trial by fire. The board had ousted his predecessor and the entire management team, and the company was undergoing an SEC investigation. The new CEO arrived amid falling employee morale, defecting customers, and media scrutiny. He resolved to quickly reinvent the company with new accounting policies, a new management team, and, eventually, a new strategic direction. But he soon realized that the company's directors, having been burned by the previous management, were keeping the company (and him) under much tighter control. It became evident that the board wanted to temper and closely monitor his actions. He immediately concluded he had to work carefully with the directors, trying his ideas on them early to get their support. Although this took more of his time than he had ever anticipated, he gradually earned their trust and was then able to move more quickly. While this example may be extreme, its lesson is applicable to all CEOs: At the end of the day, the board—not the CEO—is in charge.

As the CEO develops his boardroom relationships, he must view the directors as neither friends nor confidants (though some of them may eventually play those roles), but as bosses who hold him personally accountable for the success of the company. By actively investing in director knowledge and relationships—through one-on-one contacts, e-mail updates of corporate progress, and distribution of background material, for example—the best CEOs turn board meetings into participatory discussions rather than show-and-tell sessions by management. A new CEO who is open with—and creates the opportunity to collaborate with—his directors will be more likely to garner support from these bosses.

Surprise Six: Pleasing Shareholders Is Not the Goal

Upon taking office, new CEOs often mistakenly believe that their primary responsibility is to keep the shareholders happy. After all, shareholder value is the mantra that has defined corporate goals for many years. Courting the favor of analysts and shareholders seems natural, and every CEO (especially a new one) likes an endorsement of his leadership through a higher share price.

The problem is that defining one's goal as shareholder approval may not be in the company's best interest. Actions and strategies favored by shareholders (and analysts) may not benefit the ultimate competitive position of the company. Shareholders come and go—the average share of stock in the United States is held for less than a year—and they care only about what happens to the stock during the period they expect to own it. Analysts are naturally concerned with moving in and out of a stock, not holding it. They tend to reinforce trends—and love deals—rather than reward a long-term focus. In fact, both shareholders and analysts are prone to take a short-term view. CEOs, however, need to concern themselves with creating sustainable economic value.

Sometimes the pressure from analysts and shareholders can get so strong that it becomes destructive. One CEO in our workshop said he'd felt compelled to spin off a major division—a dramatic step that appeased analysts in the short term. Unfortunately, it hurt the longer-term performance of the company because the sale of this division drove away some customers who were vital to the growth of other divisions.

An involved, informed board can be the CEO's best ally in staying focused on the long run. The CEO of a major retailer described the perfect storm he was stepping into when he took office: a mature industry, the seemingly unconquerable Wal-Mart, and a lackluster economy. As the CEO described it, the business was badly broken, and he needed time to restore it to its former success. He worked with the board to develop a new strategy focused on regaining market share. After two quarters of heavy lifting, results began to improve. The board was pleased and employees were energized, but the analysts remained conspicuously bearish. They saw the new strategy as being too slow and drawn out. After a number of time-consuming and fruitless meetings with them, the CEO came to understand that the analysts were interested only in immediate, dramatic change—regardless of the long-run effects on the company. As he told us, "There comes a time when you just don't give a damn what the analysts think." This CEO was able to keep the focus where it needed to be because he had worked hard to ensure that his board bought into the long-term merits of the turnaround strategy.

Rather than attempt to please all shareholders through the inevitable ups and downs, CEOs must recognize that, ultimately, it is only long-term profitability that matters, not today's growth expectations or even the stock price. A high stock price will eventually collapse without the underpinnings of fundamental competitive advantage. Instead of looking to shareholders for strategic direction, the CEO must develop and articulate a clear strategy to distinguish the company from others and address industry fundamentals. A key CEO role is to sell the strategy and shape how analysts and shareholders look at the company. CEOs should not expect that their strategies will be immediately understood or accepted; a constant stream of reiterations, explanations, and reminders will likely be necessary to affect analysts' perceptions. Success in this process maybe slow. But a CEO with the courage to develop and articulate a sound strategy, even if it is currently unpopular on Wall Street, will eventually attract the right shareholders—those who buy and hold the stock because they believe in the big-picture strategy.

Surprise Seven: You Are Still Only Human

Too often, we view CEOs in the cinematic image of indefatigable superhero. Yet they remain bound by all-too-human hopes, fears, and limits. The attention and adulation that come with the job make introspection difficult and vulnerabilities inadmissible. Workshop participants told us again and again that they needed to make a conscious effort to resist the illusion of self-importance, omnipotence, and omniscience. The executives in our workshop have been remarkably forthcoming about the personal impact of being a CEO. Invariably, they have had to come to terms with the fact that they can't do everything well. They have found it difficult and ego-bruising to accept gaps in their expertise and admit that the job is more physically and emotionally taxing than any others they have held.

Maintaining some balance between the personal and the professional is another theme that comes up repeatedly in our workshop. It's easy for a new CEO to underestimate the number and magnitude of demands that will be placed upon him. Many new CEOs are confident that they can balance their new challenges with their personal lives without too much trouble—after all, they've managed to do so in other senior management positions. However, the CEO role, with all its demands and its public nature, can significantly intensify this tension. As one CEO concluded, "In the end, there is no such thing as balance. There are only trade-offs."

The difficulties don't arise solely from time constraints. Many aspects of a CEO's life become public that most of us would prefer to keep private. One CEO told us that his teenage daughter approached him after she read a high-profile newspaper article disclosing his compensation. He had never before discussed his income with his children. Even though his pay was quite modest compared with that of his peers, he had to explain to his family why he earned what he did. Another CEO said that he was dreading the first family holiday gathering after he'd become CEO and the reactions of his siblings now that his success was so public. Virtually every new CEO reports that relationships with friends and family have changed.

It surprised us that many new CEOs—even in the early days—were already thinking about their legacies. While this can lead to a long-term focus, which is desirable, it can also lead to bold (and even reckless) attempts to make a mark on the company by changing what should be left unchanged. With such goals, it is easy to be seduced by major deals and tempting to create an organization that is three times larger even if it is less profitable.

It is essential for new CEOs to make a disciplined effort to stay humble, to revisit their decisions and actions, to continue to listen to others, and to find people who will be honest and forthright. Otherwise, the rewards and praise bestowed upon a CEO can tempt him into acts of hubris. A capable and active board can also provide a check on such temptations.

Workshop participants recognized that they needed connections to the world outside their organizations, at home and in the community, to avoid being consumed by their corporate lives. Many found personally fulfilling outlets for their human needs through public service commitments. CEOs needed and wanted some relaxation too. Regular exercise, family vacations, and golf seemed to be the preferred avenues, though one CEO even took up race car driving as a hobby. He explained that he knew he would never be Mario Andretti, but he could occupy and challenge himself by trying.

Implications for CEO Leadership

Taken together, the seven surprises carry some important and subtle implications for how a new CEO should define his job.

First, the CEO must learn to manage organizational context rather than focus on daily operations. Providing leadership in this way—and not diving into the details— can be a jarring transition. One CEO said that he initially felt like the company's "most useless executive," despite the power inherent in the job. The CEO needs to learn how to act in indirect ways—setting and communicating strategy, putting sound processes in place, selecting and mentoring key people—to create the conditions that will help others make the right choices. At the same time, he must set the tone and define the organization's culture and values through his words and actions—in other words, demonstrate how employees should behave.

Second, he must recognize that his position does not confer the right to lead, nor does it guarantee the organization's loyalty. He must perpetually earn and maintain the moral mandate to lead. CEOs can easily lose their legitimacy if their vision is unconvincing, if their actions are inconsistent with the values they espouse, or if their self-interest appears to trump the welfare of the organization. They must realize that success ultimately depends on their ability to enlist the voluntary commitment rather than the forced obedience of others. While mastering the conventional tools of management may have won the CEO his job, these tools alone will not keep him there.

Finally, the CEO must not get totally absorbed in the role. Even if others think he is omnipotent, he is still only human. Failing to recognize this will lead to arrogance, exhaustion, and a shortened tenure. Only by maintaining a personal balance and staying grounded can the CEO achieve the perspective required to make decisions in the interest of the company and its long-term prosperity.

Learning the Ropes

THE NEW CEO WORKSHOP at Harvard Business School is open only to newly appointed CEOs of companies with annual revenues of $1 billion or more. In keeping with the mission of HBS—to educate leaders who make a difference in the world—we introduced this workshop several years ago to address the distinctive challenges facing first-time chief executives in large, complex enterprises. We personally invite each participant, to ensure the appropriate size and composition of the group, which typically includes about ten CEOs whose organizations cover a broad cross section of industries. These CEOs run public companies based in advanced economies. They have been appointed and are either waiting to take office or within the first few months of tenure. Since the program's inception several years ago, about 50 new CEOs have participated, from world-leading companies such as Applied Materials, BellSouth, Cadbury Schweppes, Caterpillar, Lloyds TSB, Lowe's, Novartis, Schlumberger, UPS, and Walgreens. Recently, a group of early workshop participants reconvened to review the first several years in their jobs and to recalibrate their agendas.

The workshop offers a unique perspective from which to explore both the predictable and the surprising aspects of becoming a CEO. We interview all participants in advance, using a structured set of questions about their strategy, their relationship with the board, and their immediate and longer-term challenges. Discussion sessions during the two-day program are built around these and other areas where new CEOs face unfamiliar challenges, and around peer and faculty dialogue.

We typically start by asking the CEOs to look ahead to the end of their tenure and give their retirement speech. The next day, we ask them to describe their immediate challenges. We then closely examine some of these challenges, such as crafting a strategy that creates lasting economic value, building a productive relationship with the board of directors, communicating effectively with inside and outside constituencies, and setting the proper tone and style to create a strong culture. The sessions are extremely interactive, and discussions involve in-depth sharing of personal experiences.

The seven surprises to new CEOs described in this article are challenges highlighted again and again in our workshop discussions. The stories we use to illustrate these lessons are drawn from the experiences of participants and from our own collective experiences working with CEOs. (We are grateful to Patia McGrath, our research associate, for her help in organizing these workshops and in preparing this article.)

The Seven Things You Need to Know

MOST NEW CHIEF executives are taken aback by the unexpected and unfamiliar new roles, the time and information limitations, and the altered professional relationships they run up against. Here are the common surprises new CEOs face, and here's how to tell when adjustments are necessary.

Surprise One: You Can't Run the Company

Warning Signs:

- You are in too many meetings and involved in too many tactical discussions.

- There are too many days when you feel as though you have lost control over your time.

Surprise Two: Giving Orders Is Very Costly
Warning Signs:

- You have become the bottleneck.
- Employees are overly inclined to consult you before they act.
- People start using your name to endorse things, as in, "Frank says..."

Surprise Three: It Is Hard to Know What Is Really Going On
Warning Signs:

- You keep hearing things that surprise you.
- You learn about events after the fact.
- You hear concerns and dissenting views through the grapevine rather than directly.

Surprise Four: You Are Always Sending a Message
Warning Signs:

- Employees circulate stories about your behavior that magnify or distort reality.
- People around you act in ways that indicate they're trying to anticipate your likes and dislikes.

Surprise Five: You Are Not the Boss
Warning Signs:

- You don't know where you stand with board members.

- Roles and responsibilities of the board members and of management are not clear.
- The discussions in board meetings are limited mostly to reporting on results and management's decisions.

Surprise Six: Pleasing Shareholders Is Not the Goal
Warning Signs:

- Executives and board members judge actions by their effect on stock price.
- Analysts who don't understand the business push for decisions that risk the health of the company.
- Management incentives are disproportionately tied to stock price.

Surprise Seven: You Are Still Only Human
Warning Signs:

- You give interviews about you rather than about the company.
- Your lifestyle is more lavish or privileged than that of other top executives in the company.
- You have few if any activities not connected to the company.

Originally published in October 2004
Reprint R0410C

Almost Ready

How Leaders Move Up

DAN CIAMPA

Executive Summary

MOST DESIGNATED CEO SUCCESSORS are talented, hardworking, and smart enough to go all the way—yet fail to land the top job. What they don't realize is, the qualities that helped them in their climb to the number two position aren't enough to boost them to number one.

In addition to running their businesses well, the author explains, would-be CEOs must master the art of forming coalitions and winning support. They must also sharpen their self-awareness and their sensitivity to the needs of bosses and influential peers because they typically receive little performance feedback once they're on track to become CEO. Indeed, the ability to pick up on subtle cues is often an important part of the test.

When succession doesn't go well—or fails altogether—many people pay the price: employees depending on a smooth handoff at the top, investors expecting continuous leadership, and families uprooted when jobs don't pan out. Among those at fault are boards that do not keep a close watch on the succession process, human resource organizations that should have the capacity to help but are not up to the task, and CEOs who do a poor job coaching potential successors.

But the aspiring CEO also bears some responsibility. He can dramatically increase his chances of success by understanding his boss's point of view, knowing his own limitations, and managing what psychologist Gerry Egan has called the "shadow organization"—the political side of a company, characterized by unspoken relationships and alliances—without being labeled "political." Most of all, he must learn to conduct himself with a level of maturity and wisdom that signals he is ready—not almost ready—to be chief executive.

SHORTLY AFTER BEING elected U.S. president in 1960, John Kennedy offered Robert McNamara, then president of Ford, the post of treasury secretary. McNamara turned down the offer, saying he wasn't qualified for the job. Then, Kennedy offered him the job of secretary of defense. When McNamara demurred again for the same reason, a frustrated Kennedy exclaimed: "Bob, there is no school to learn to be president, either!"

Leadership at the top is never easy for even the most experienced people. For someone taking on the job of

CEO for the first time, mastering the new skills and sorting out the uncertainties that go with the position can be an overwhelming challenge. So it should come as no surprise that the corner suite has a revolving door. The Center for Creative Leadership has estimated that 40% of new CEOs fail in their first 18 months. What's more, the churn rate is on the rise: In a 2002 study, the center found that the number of CEOs leaving their jobs had increased 10% since 2001. As a recent report from the outplacement firm Challenger, Gray & Christmas points out, "The biggest challenge looming over corporate America [is] finding replacement CEOs."

That's a problem for aspiring chief executives. Look at what we know about the experiences of designated CEO successors—talented and hardworking executives who were successful at each stage in their climb to the number two position. Research conducted in the 1990s (by Michael Watkins, of Harvard Business School, and me) showed that, when promoted from within an organization, less than half the people who reached the number two spot expecting to win the CEO title actually ended up in the position. We also saw more organizations going outside their own ranks to hire designated successors— but disturbingly, once hired, only one-quarter of these candidates were successful at either being named CEO or at staying in the CEO job for more than two years.

Clearly, there is an urgent need for CEOs and boards of directors to have an efficient and effective succession process, but few do. While HR departments should be driving the process, most have neither the skills to translate best practices nor the credibility with boards to make an impact. Many corporations—even family-owned businesses, where the financial security of generations is at stake—don't even get as far as having a plan.

A 2002 survey by the MassMutual Financial Group and the George and Robin Raymond Family Business Institute showed that although 40% of the polled chairmen and CEOs planned to retire within four years, 55% of the ones age 61 or older had not settled on a succession plan.

But would-be CEOs must also bear responsibility for their success. All too often, they fail to recognize that the qualities they must demonstrate to make the leap from likely successor to CEO are different from the skills they relied on to get to the number two position. In addition to excelling at running their businesses, aspiring CEOs must master the art of forming coalitions and winning the support of people who are competitors. These are elements of what psychologist Gerry Egan has called the "shadow organization"—the political side of a company, characterized by unspoken relationships, alliances, and influence exerted by coalitions. Because, in most cases, aspiring CEOs receive little actionable feedback once they become designated successors, they must sharpen their self-awareness as well as their sensitivity to the wants and needs of bosses and influential peers; they must learn to conduct themselves with a level of maturity and wisdom that signals to boards as well as CEOs that they are ready—not just almost ready—to be chief executive.

The CEO Succession Difference

How is top-level succession unique? To answer that question, take the case of Dennis (names in examples throughout this article have been changed). Dennis was on the fast track from the start. An Ivy League graduate, he spent three years in an industry leader's sales-training program, got his MBA at a top school, and completed a finance-training program in another industry-leading company. After 18 months, he moved to the marketing department there, then to a branch manager job for a few years. Next, he jumped to a competitor to become a country manager ("I had to get my international ticket punched"); sales records were set in his market. Five years later, he was named senior vice president for emerging markets.

Not long after that, Dennis left to become the designated CEO successor at a company in a different industry, where he was unfamiliar with the products and technology. "I wasn't looking," he said, "but I knew I could run something bigger. I was ready. I was 44 years old, and [the COO and CEO of the company I had left] were in their midfifties . . . and there were some talented people between me and them. Leaving there was the way to be a CEO faster." In business school, he had set a goal to become a CEO by age 50. "As I got closer to the top, I became more confident that I'd reach that goal. I had been in four successful companies where I'd seen CEOs up close. I'm not saying that I'm better than they were, but I knew I could do their job."

The succession plan approved by the board was for Dennis to enter as COO, with marketing, sales, manufacturing, engineering, and service reporting to him while the senior staff people (the head of HR, the CFO, and the general counsel) plus R&D stayed under Harvey, the chairman and CEO. The role of president remained unfilled. If things went well over the first 18 months, Dennis would take on that title. In another year, he would become CEO, and six months after that, Harvey would retire.

While successful over the years, Dennis's new company had seen its growth rate slow as market share eroded. "It was all about the numbers," Dennis said. "I was brought in because everyone knew I'd find a way to make them. I didn't need to know the technology as long as I could take cost out, manage the brand, and get service to be more responsive. It was right up my alley." In less than 18 months, he rationalized manufacturing, reorganized to speed up decision making, replaced many people he believed could not perform at a higher level, and helped the balance sheet through a new just-in-time inventory program. He admitted that there was more resistance to changes than he had anticipated and that Harvey had recommended moving forward more gradually and involving some of the older managers to a greater degree. Dennis complained to me: "I filled [Harvey] in on everything, and he never said no. . . . He could have vetoed any of these things, but he never did. . . . He knew that they would pay off."

But before Dennis was there two years, Harvey asked for his resignation, saying that things just hadn't worked out as everyone had hoped. He said that he and the board had decided to promote the CFO to president. Harvey did not give Dennis any feedback, explaining that there "really would be no purpose served" in doing so. He added that Dennis had brought much value for the shareholders and should feel good about what he had accomplished—that he was still young and would be a CEO somewhere.

Although the company provided a generous severance package, Dennis was angry, contending that he had been misled and used. I asked him why he believed he had failed to get the job he had so carefully prepared for. "You know, Dan," he replied, "I did all the right things . . . the things the business needed. To me, it was all because of politics. The engineering guy and the head of manufacturing and [the head] of R&D were all against the changes that I was making. . . . They wanted to keep things the way they were so they could hold on to their power . . . and they turned people against me. And Harvey doesn't like conflict. He could have told these guys to get with the plan, but he avoided that because it was going to be a tough conversation."

Dennis is a talented executive, but his reaction is a sign of why he failed. He is unlikely to reach his goal until he stops blaming others and considers what he did or did not do to cause his predicament. To start with, his conviction that making the numbers is what it takes to secure the top job is off the mark. While this is important, it's not enough to differentiate one talented CEO candidate from another. Also, Dennis's time as COO was not meant to showcase the abilities that got him to the number two spot. Rather, it was a test of his ability to manage his most important relationships and alliances. In a sense, therefore, Dennis was right—politics undid him. But political skills are essential for a CEO. Dennis neglected to see that he needed other people's help to succeed at this level and that his test was to prove he was capable of embracing a new culture, finding value in it, and appreciating perspectives other than his own. Dennis was also wrong to expect Harvey to clear away the opposition—or even to point to its existence. Understanding who must be won over to your point of view is a key part of managing the succession process.

Pitfalls of CEO Succession

When CEO hopefuls concentrate on doing more of what they have done to succeed, they typically spend too little time cultivating important relationships, especially with their bosses. Consider Vince, a manager who turned around the largest division of a struggling consumer company in less than a year. The company had developed a corporate culture where length of service counted more than performance. Vince made progress toward a performance mentality by replacing some of the people who most resisted change and introducing a performance measurement system that made it clear to those in his organization what was expected of them. At the same time, his informal style and accessibility conveyed to people that he valued them and their contributions. Employees quickly came to trust Vince and lined up behind him and what he wanted to do.

The trouble was that Vince never developed a relationship with his boss. Their regular one-on-one meetings soon became mechanical, and over time, Vince even gave up preparing for them. "He doesn't talk about strategic things. He just does check-ins on what I'm already doing," Vince complained. "It's like he thinks I'm not taking care of these things." After 18 months, discouraged that the CEO was not treating him as a successor, Vince was looking for another job. He had not stopped to analyze what the CEO paid attention to or expected from senior people. In particular, he didn't grasp that it was more important to develop a relationship with his boss than it was for his boss to create one with him. Vince didn't understand that his test was to show that he was perceptive and flexible enough to adapt to his boss's style, which differed from what he was accustomed to.

Even if would-be CEOs succeed in relating well to their bosses, some don't display enough ability to "elevate"—in other words, to gain the perspective expected of CEOs. Consider Leigh, a talented executive who had risen internally through a succession of operating

management jobs in a technology-dependent manufacturing company. Because she was not an engineer, Leigh
had to work harder and be more prepared than most of
her technically trained peers. Although she saw it as
unfair, she admitted that it had "made me a more complete, well-rounded manager. . . . I had to learn a lot
more just to get my job done because I wasn't sure I
could get support [I needed]." Her hard work and
uncomplaining style were noticed by the CEO years
before Leigh was promoted to the number two spot. "I
knew what she was going through," the CEO said, "but
she never showed how difficult it was for her. I think it
made her tougher, more mature. . . . It broadened her;
she was learning two or three jobs at a time, not just one."

But soon after Leigh became COO, her boss began to
wonder whether she could handle the top job. "I didn't
worry that she couldn't handle the men she beat out
[now peers or subordinates] or that they'd resist doing
what she told them. . . . They understood Leigh's
strengths as well as I did. It's because I was not sure if
she could elevate." He went on to describe complaints
from Leigh's managers about not having enough free-
dom to run their operations. "[Her] being too controlling
wasn't my experience with her, so I checked it out
myself. I found out that she was jumping in to solve the
problems rather than making sure her people solved
them. Doing things herself was the way she had gotten
ahead, but she didn't understand that at this level it was
going to drag her into too much detail. If a task force was
not moving fast enough, she would meet with it to get
things moving instead of staying above it, laying out
what had to happen, and holding the leader of the committee accountable. It was the same with her [direct
reports]. If one of them came to her with a problem,

she'd give him the answer instead of guiding him to find it himself." Although Leigh was "running a real tight ship, and all the right things were happening, the way she operated kept her from looking out three or four years, seeing where our [technological] edge was threatened, asking what [our major competitor] was doing that we hadn't thought about yet, and really testing her people to see if they could step up to the next level."

If they had been filled in regarding their bosses' concerns, both Vince and Leigh could have turned their situations around. But when it was suggested that Leigh's boss give her feedback, he said unenthusiastically, "I may mention it to her." Vince's boss said, "No, I want to see if Vince gets it on his own." These reactions underline a subtle reality of life at this level: Would-be CEOs can't expect much help in moving to the top spot. Boards and chief executives will give only the slightest indications of the behavior they expect. It is not that they want the number two to come in knowing all the answers. Rather, they want to see whether a candidate is sensitive to subtle cues and can adjust her behavior accordingly. CEOs and chairmen are more likely to test than to counsel.

Cue awareness is more than window dressing when it comes to trying to win the number one spot. That's because relationships at the top are so heavily scrutinized and the aspiring CEO is always in the spotlight. At this level, a senior manager gets an edge by being concerned with what is best for the whole company as well as with what's good for the units that report to her. Take Helen, a leader in a large, global corporation at the head of its industry. Some saw her as the logical successor to the CEO. She had strong interpersonal skills complemented by charm and humility—rare qualities in her company. Her climb up the ladder was swift; in her mid-forties, she was reporting to the CEO and running the most profitable part of the corporation. That's when Helen's career plateaued.

Her CEO explained that she was "important to this company in so many ways, but one big reason that she could probably never be a CEO was the downside of loyalty." Although she often talked about the need for teamwork among her peers, she didn't always act as a team player. She made loyalty to her and her agenda the price of admission to her inner circle. She resisted allowing her better people to move to other parts of the corporation, especially if it meant they would be working for another CEO contender. The CEO had a few concerns about her. First, her behavior revealed that she cared more about the success of her own unit than about the success of the organization overall. Second, she kept her better people from jobs in other areas of the company, denying them chances to broaden themselves and robbing other departments of new talent. Third, while she enjoyed intense loyalty within her organization, she had not gained the political support from her peers she would need as CEO, nor had she seeded other parts of the organization with people who knew her well and could help her when she needed it.

Good CEOs and boards are experts at assessing an aspiring CEO's ability to master the nuances of the top job. For Dennis, the test was to find value in the culture of the company whose performance he was improving; for Vince, to gauge what was important to his boss; for Leigh, to point people toward solutions rather than solving all the problems herself; and for Helen, to help others succeed and to concentrate on improving the organization as a whole, not just her unit. These potential successors did not understand the tests they faced, so they missed subtle cues and were set back in their quest for the top position.

Winning Criteria

Each of the designated successors in the examples above failed to establish sufficient credibility for their bosses to stand aside. The signs that they were failing were not easy for them to recognize because they were well matched with the strategic and technical needs of their jobs; indeed, these people were talented, accomplished managers who contributed much to their organizations. What extra ingredients should they have brought? What criteria should CEOs and boards use in judging CEO candidates? (For a more complete list, see the exhibit "The Winner's Difference.")

The Winner's Difference

The following table lists the capabilities of people who have a good chance of becoming CEO—and what elite candidates do in addition in order to get the edge.

	The Good Candidate:	The Elite Candidate:
Management Savvy	• knows what is required operationally for short-term results • motivates others to do it	• avoids jumping in personally to solve problems others can handle
	• uses time well • prioritizes among issues that are all important	• makes the right judgments about what to expend energy on
	• frequently delegates tasks • has a history of developing subordinates and exporting talent	• maintains control of the key decisions and a full pipeline of talented people
	• organizes and mobilizes talent toward most significant problems • pushes people to achieve more than they think they can	• makes people feel appreciated and stay loyal

Political Intelligence	• accurately reads political currents	• isn't labeled "political"
	• understands patterns of relationships quickly in an unfamiliar environment	• recognizes how relationships are likely to affect early success
	• builds relationships with peers and subordinates	• gets peers and subordinates to go out of their way to help
	• makes sure the CEO and the board know what he or she is capable of doing	• doesn't seem self-serving
Personal Style	• is a star performer	• makes success look effortless
	• is intense and driven to excel	• allows others' performance to be recognized, too
	• is hardworking, usually putting in more time and effort than peers do	• manages energy to stay on the "rested edge" and to avoid the "ragged edge"
	• enthusiastically backs initiatives that will help the business succeed	• knows when to hold back and when to let go
	• is a leader among peers	• enables peers to improve their performance
	• understands new ways of doing things and makes important connections	• stays grounded and makes sure basic needs are met while mastering new concepts

Watching and analyzing successes and failures at the number two level suggests that executives vary in the degree to which they have the qualifications to win the top job. At one end of the spectrum are managers who have the capabilities they need to be considered as CEOs. Managers on the other end, however, are the elite few who have honed these capabilities with the subtlety and sophistication required for operating effectively at the CEO level.

The capabilities fall into a few broad categories. The first set has to do with senior management best practices—for example, the ability to prioritize the things that will make the difference operationally. At this level, managers must use time wisely, delegate the right tasks, and develop people; these are basic abilities expected of everyone. But the people who make it to the top tend to proceed in subtly different ways than do the senior managers who remain stuck at number two. For instance, winners know what is required for short-term results, and they can direct others to do it. But unlike Leigh, they avoid getting too involved in solving problems that others should handle.

The second set of capabilities has to do with managing the political environment. At the less-sophisticated end of the spectrum are those who accurately read most political currents, while those with better-honed abilities will do so in a way that avoids their being labeled "political." Most senior executives build good working relationships with peers (which Helen did), but the ones who become CEOs garner active peer support. Often, their peers and subordinates will go out of their way to offer feedback or to point out potential problems (which Helen's colleagues didn't do). Most people close to the top also know how to show the CEO and the board what they are capable of doing. But the ones who don't make it to the number one job tend to believe that they haven't received the recognition they deserve. (This is true of both Vince and Dennis.) As a result, they come across as too concerned with getting credit. Executives at the other end of the continuum receive credit by finding ways for their virtues to be touted by others, so they don't need to shine the spotlight of attention too brightly on themselves. The third category has to do with personal style. The number two works hard, sacrificing personal time and expending significant effort to achieve impressive results. But the winner never makes a big deal of the success he is responsible for (unlike Dennis and Vince). Of course, being intensely competitive and driven to be the best is a given among high-level managers, but those who are furthest along the spectrum manage to give credit to others involved in successes without diminishing their own recognition. Being a leader among peers is what all senior executives have done to get where they are; elite executives have learned how to do it so that their peers become better performers.

Rules of Engagement

Success at winning the CEO title always depends on the situation, the organizational culture, the types of people and relationships involved, and the personality and style of the candidate. While there are no hard-and-fast rules, a few basic guidelines can help the aspiring CEO shape his own destiny.

UNDERSTAND THE BOSS'S POINT OF VIEW

Whether the CEO has earned your respect is not the issue here. All that matters is that you respect his position and get to know what is important to him. Start by understanding what contributed most to his success: Who helped him along the way, and are those advisers still valuable to him? How did he handle failures?

Then try to understand the type of person he is. What is his leadership style and approach to decision making? What types of questions does he ask? Does he ask questions to verify what he has concluded or to gain input he has not considered? How does he respond to the answers? Does he tend to make decisions by talking with people one-on-one or in a group? Also, search for clues that indicate the best way to relate to him. Which people influence him the most? How does he manage their advice? How does he want to be kept informed? What behavior does he expect from senior people? How does the boss's style differ from yours and from the styles of others you have worked for?

It's essential to appreciate how difficult it is for him to hand over the reins. Years ago, I was the designated successor for a CEO who I believe was passing the chairman and CEO titles to me only reluctantly. I was determined to work harder and be more productive so he would have no excuse to back away. The founder of the Boston Consulting Group, Bruce Henderson (who had retired and thus gone through his own transfer of power to a successor), was one of my advisers. When I asked him for feedback on what I should be doing differently, I expected a pearl of strategic wisdom about accelerating top-line growth to increase our market share. But he simply said, "Be more understanding about what [the chairman] is going through." Instead of thinking that Bruce had lost a bit of his edge and being disappointed that he did not say something about what I was going through, I should have taken the time to understand what he meant. If I had, my transition would have gone more smoothly.

KNOW YOUR LIMITATIONS

There are many incentives for board members, CEOs, HR people, or executive search consultants to encourage a potential CEO to believe that he is more prepared than he really is. While these people are often well-intentioned, if he believes them, he might pay too little attention to cultivating the particular abilities most important for his success.

Take the case of Wayne, who moved from a *Fortune 50* global corporation to a smaller company because of the opportunity to become CEO years earlier than if he had stayed put. The incumbent chairman and CEO was ill, and the lead director of the board had taken over most of his duties. Wayne was recruited aggressively by the board members, partly because he had much of what they believed their company needed, but also because the corporation where he had become a rising star was among the world's best performers and was known for producing very good managers. The board reasoned that Wayne would impress investors and employees alike.

In his first year after joining, Wayne worked hard to master new technologies, markets, and customers. He learned how to impress analysts and institutional investors. His operational skills turned out to be just what the company needed, bringing remarkable bottom-line results and cost savings. His upbeat style was refreshing, and his encouragement to try new approaches motivated employees to innovate at a rate the company had not seen before. After 11 months, the lead director said, "The board believes things are going really well and wants to accelerate your move up to CEO. . . . You're our guy."

Wayne was surprised, pleased, and anxious all at the same time. He appreciated the vote of confidence, but, although he took care not to appear as though he believed the top job exceeded his capabilities, he was unsure that he was ready for such a step. He was still learning the business, and there were challenges (such as acquisitions and technical alliances) with which he had little direct experience and where the managers in charge had not impressed him.

Over the next month, several of the directors spent more time meeting with Wayne than they had in his entire tenure at the company. At first he thought they were testing him, but he soon realized that they were trying to persuade him to take the CEO spot. They were selling.

Wayne lasted 15 months as CEO. He was not ready and should have stayed in the number two spot for another couple of years. It is difficult to blame him for taking the opportunity to be CEO—his failure was really more the fault of the board. Eventually, he would have had the self-confidence and experience to be very effective as head of that company. The board members were more concerned about image and getting someone in the CEO spot quickly. In other words, they cared more about what was good for the board than about what was good for Wayne or even the company.

MANAGE THE SHADOW ORGANIZATION

In order to get a CEO position, it's important to grasp the alliances and political realities that aren't apparent right away but come with top-level jobs. Whether entering a new organization or being promoted to headquarters, the wise manager will find ways to understand how this often-hidden network of relationships and norms can influence her success.

One way to gain such understanding is to trace the histories of successes and failures. Who were the people most responsible, and what happened to them? How did they help form influential groups? What patterns of loyalty emerged? Were there attempts to isolate lessons and ensure they were understood? Is such learning reflected in who has been hired, in performance management, and in training and development programs? In getting to the core of reality, it is useful to look to Japanese manufacturers of the 1970s. They adopted the habit of asking "why" five times when they discovered an important production or distribution problem, because they believed that root causes lay at least four levels below the surface.

Another way to grasp the political climate is to understand what is actually valued. Most CEOs have endorsed a list of values that are prominently displayed on office walls. In most cases, though, these bear little resemblance to actual behavior or to how the most important decisions are made. To determine whether values are meaningful, find out how they came into existence. They mean something when they have been created over a long period, evolving from ethical wins and mistakes. They stand the test of time. The most cherished are passed from one generation to the next. Values are sure to be superficial, however, when they have been created by outsiders for a fee. Here is a particularly ironic example: One company unveiled a new set of values written by a consulting firm that in the same week admitted its role in another client's financial scandal.

Most people who get close to the top are talented, hardworking, and smart enough to go all the way—but fail because they don't know how to approach this entirely new challenge. A good number of these failures are avoidable. That we have allowed this to happen in organizations that are otherwise excellent performers is a disgrace; it exacts a huge cost in terms of time, money, and wasted potential. The price is paid by many people: employees depending on a smooth handoff at the top, investors expecting continuous leadership, and families uprooted when jobs do not work out as hoped. Among those at fault are boards of directors that do not oversee the succession process or hold CEOs accountable for a smooth transition, human resource organizations that should have the capacity to help but are not up to the task, and CEOs who do a poor job of coaching potential successors.

In spite of these obstacles, the aspiring CEO can dramatically increase his chances of success by sharpening his perception of the organization's culture and politics, by mastering the art of building winning relationships, and by improving his self-awareness. Most of all, he must learn to conduct himself with the maturity and wisdom that demonstrate to those making the decision that he is, indeed, ready.

Originally published in January 2005
Reprint R0501D

Surviving Your New CEO

KEVIN P. COYNE AND EDWARD J. COYNE, SR.

Executive Summary

ALMOST 50% OF THE LARGEST American firms
will have a new CEO within the next four years;
your company could very well be next. Senior
executives know that a CEO transition means
they're in for a round of firings, organizational
reshuffles, and other unwelcome career changes.
When your career suddenly depends on the views
of a person you may not know, how worried
should you be?

According to the authors—very. They investigated the 2002–2004 CEO turnover rates of the
top 1,000 U.S. companies and interviewed more
than a dozen CEOs, each of whom had taken
over at least one very large organization. Their
study reveals that when a new CEO takes charge,

remaining top managers are more likely than not to be shown the door. Those who leave often land in a lower position at a new company, work in a much smaller firm, or retire altogether. The news is not all grim, however. The interviewees offer some pointers on how to create a good impression and maximize your chances of survival and success under the new regime.

Some of that advice may surprise you. One CEO pointed out, for instance, that "managers do not realize how much the CEO is looking for teammates on day one. I am amazed at how few people come through the door and say, 'I want to help. I may not be perfect, but I buy into your vision.'" Other recommendations are more intuitive, such as learning the new CEO's working style, understanding her agenda, and helping her look good in her new position by achieving positive operating results—and soon.

Along with the inevitable stresses, the authors point out, CEO transitions can provide opportunities. Whether you reinvigorate your career within your company or find fulfillment elsewhere, the key lies in deciding what you want to do—and then doing it right.

T HE HIGH TURNOVER of CEOs in the United States affects huge numbers of other executives. At the current rate, almost 50% of the largest American firms will have a new CEO within the next four years. Another 25,000 newly acquired companies will also report to new leaders. If you're a senior team member in a firm with a new

chief executive, your career now depends on the views
of a person you may not know. What's more, your history
of successes and failures may not count for much.
"Remember that you are starting over," says the
internally appointed CEO of a top-ten U.S. insurance
company. "No matter what your track record was—hey,
it's different now."

Anecdotal stories of what happens to executive teams
during CEO transitions are hardly comforting. Firings,
organizational reshuffles, and canceled strategies result
in abrupt and unwelcome career changes for a host of
senior managers. If you're faced with a new CEO, three
questions probably loom very large in your mind: How
worried should I be? What will happen to me if I do get
pushed out? If I stay on, what should I do to maximize
the chances of prospering with my new boss?

To answer these questions, we built databases compil-
ing rates of CEO and other high-level executive turnover
from 2002 to 2004 at the top 1,000 U.S. companies, as determined by their market cap at the end of 2001 (see the sidebar "About the Research"). We also investigated the most
recently reported employment status of executives who
had left companies with new CEOs during that time. In
addition, we interviewed more than a dozen CEOs who
had taken over at least one very large company. Because
of the nature of our research, the results we compiled are
not absolute. By studying several constellations of data,
however, we were able to make inferences about the
effects of CEO turnover on executives.

One conclusion, in particular, is striking: Chances
are high that executives will find themselves out the
door. They're more likely than not to land in a lower
position at a new company, to work in a much smaller
firm, or to retire altogether. Despite this grim picture,

our interviews with CEOs revealed steps you can take to survive and even thrive, depending on how you behave in the first few days, weeks, and months of the new leader's tenure. Taken to heart, this practical advice may help you stay on board.

The Fate of Executives

To see what happens when a new chief executive takes over, we examined the turnover rates of proxy-level managers and other senior leaders in firms that maintained the status quo, promoted someone to CEO from within the company, or hired a new CEO from outside the company. We'll start with proxy-level executives.

First, we looked at companies where the CEO remained constant. Proxy-level senior management turnover under those circumstances had a weighted average of 16% annually. Roughly half (about 8.5%) was voluntary, consisting of people who retired or who faced health or family issues, and that rate appeared to be unaffected by the company's performance. More important is the rate of involuntary turnover, including firings and unplanned early retirements. This averaged about 7.5% overall, with slight differences depending on how well the company was performing.

Next, we looked at the turnover rates for companies in which an internal executive had moved up the corporate ladder to the top spot. In such cases, the news was generally bad: The rate of involuntary turnover jumped up to 12.5%—an increase of about 65%. When we included voluntary turnover as well, the chances of a senior executive's leaving grew to more than one in five.

Then we considered cases in which the new CEO came from outside the company, which generally happens only in midperforming and low-performing firms (high-performing companies almost never replace their CEOs with outsiders). Here, the story gets much worse: Involuntary turnover averaged a whopping 26%— almost four times the rate when the CEO did not change. A further breakdown revealed that the involuntary turnover rate at companies with average performance was 24%, while the rate at poorly performing companies was 31%. Thus, overall, if you are listed in the proxy statement and your company brings in an outside CEO after a year of subpar performance, you have about a two in five chance of leaving your job.

What about other senior executives? The pattern for them was very similar to that for proxy-level executives but slightly less worrisome. On average, turnover among all executive officers rose only a little when the new CEO came from within the company but quite a lot when the CEO came from outside. In the latter situation, more than 25% left within a year, and the odds of an involuntary departure more than doubled (see the exhibit "When a New CEO Enters, Executives Exit").

What happens to executives who leave? Is losing their job, as the cliché goes, "the best thing that ever happened to them"? Do they in fact land on their feet, or do they suffer massive career setbacks?

An executive who has been doing a good job may assume that even if he is asked to leave, he will find an equal or better job elsewhere and so may tend to be relaxed about his fate under the new leader. Unfortunately, the data do not support this optimistic outlook. Of the approximately 400 proxy-level executives who left following the arrival of a new CEO in 2002 or 2003, none moved to a proxy-level job in any large U.S. firm. (To be fair, very few proxy-level executives who departed a company where the CEO remained constant found comparable jobs elsewhere either—but that's cold comfort.)

When a New CEO Enters, Executives Exit

Annual turnover among senior managers jumps dramatically when a new CEO takes the helm—particularly if he or she comes from outside the firm.

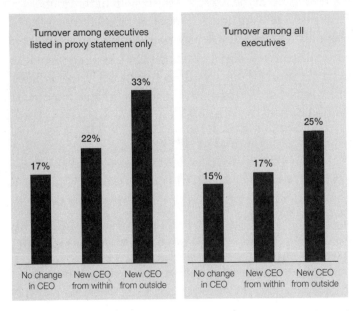

Turnover among executives listed in proxy statement only

- No change in CEO: 17%
- New CEO from within: 22%
- New CEO from outside: 33%

Turnover among all executives

- No change in CEO: 15%
- New CEO from within: 17%
- New CEO from outside: 25%

Unweighted percentages based on a study of executive turnover in the top 1,000 U.S. companies, 2002–2004.

The broader group of exiting executives generally fared poorly, too. We discovered this by comparing their previous companies and job titles with their new ones. We separated the executives into four categories— *winners, laterals, setbacks,* and *dropouts*—based on the combination of changes in their titles and the size of their employers. For example, a person who acquired a higher title at a slightly smaller firm might be classified as a lateral, but someone who accepted a lesser title at a much smaller firm would be classified as a setback.

Once again, the results are sobering. Winners were rare—only 4% of executives fell into this category. Twenty-eight percent fell into the laterals category (we gave former executives now serving exclusively as board members—almost a third of the laterals—the benefit of the doubt). Three percent were designated setbacks. Fully 65%—the dropouts—moved to sole proprietorships or companies with sales of less than $10 million (22%), or disappeared from our source databases altogether (43%). It seems likely that this last group either retired or moved quite far down the corporate ladder (see the exhibit "The Prospering Few").

The Prospering Few

Senior managers who leave their jobs following a CEO replacement can be sorted into four categories: Winners *accept a better position at a similarly sized company or keep the same title but move to a larger company.* Laterals *accept a lesser title at a larger company, maintain their former level at a similarly sized company, or take a better position at a smaller company.* Setbacks *accept a lesser position at a similarly sized or smaller company or keep their former title at a smaller company.* Dropouts *either join an extremely small venture or disappear from the corporate radar screen altogether.*

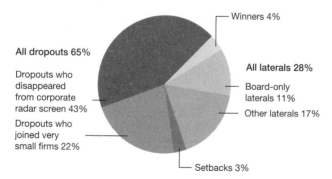

All dropouts 65%

Dropouts who disappeared from corporate radar screen 43%

Dropouts who joined very small firms 22%

Winners 4%

All laterals 28%

Board-only laterals 11%

Other laterals 17%

Setbacks 3%

Based on a study of executive turnover in the top 1,000 U.S. companies, 2002–2004.

Younger executives may be tempted to believe that they stand a better chance of surviving than those closer to retirement age. Unfortunately, this is not the case. The overall pattern of success and failure for executives under the age of 52 is strikingly similar to the one for their older colleagues.

Given these outcomes, it's clear that you would do well to try to keep your job under the new CEO—after all, you have nothing to lose. Your survival, however, may depend on whether you take the steps described below.

How to Survive

Every new CEO makes people decisions quickly: On average, the ones we interviewed said they had made final determinations about their teams within 60 days, even when they had publicly vowed to take their time. The statement of one well-known CEO at a $10 billion services company, for example, is typical. When asked at his initial press conference whether there would be changes at the top, he replied that each member is valuable until proven otherwise and that making such a decision always takes a long time. Also typical is what occurred about a month later: He fired the CFO, who had put in a less-than-stellar appearance at an analysts' meeting.

Early impressions count—more than you know or maybe believe they should. New CEOs don't tend to seek input from their predecessors, and they place little weight on the input they do receive. Rather, they rely on their instincts. Since it's relatively rare for a board of directors to restrict a CEO's ability to change the management team, the impression you create with your new boss is critical.

Assuming that no force majeure exists to make your exit inevitable—for example, you're the CFO and the new leader brings along her own financial officer—how can you make a good first impression and maximize your chances of survival and success? We asked our CEO interviewees to look back on the earliest days of their new jobs and recall instances in which an executive's actions or behavior determined his or her fate. Did the executive do something to turn a negative impression into a positive one? Alternatively, did an otherwise good executive do—or fail to do—something that brought about his or her own downfall? We summarize their recommendations below.

SHOW YOUR GOODWILL

It may be tempting to wait and see what the new CEO wants of you instead of taking the initiative to talk about your responsibilities, but this is the wrong approach. Most of the CEOs we interviewed indicated that too many executives doomed themselves from the start simply by failing to manifest a willingness to be part of the new team. As the chief executive of a $20 billion industrial company put it, "Managers do not realize how much the CEO is looking for teammates on day one. I am amazed at how few people come through the door and say, 'I want to help. I may not be perfect, but I buy into your vision.' That alone makes a huge difference." Another CEO was even more frank: "Virtually no one came to see me to ask how they could help. It is naive and stupid for managers to hold back and be guarded."

It is also dangerous to assume that your new CEO already understands that you want to cooperate. According to our interviewees, the exiting executives who opposed the new CEO's program never once announced their opposition—so the leaders certainly did not equate silence with agreement. In the absence of strong signals, CEOs draw their own conclusions about your views. If those conclusions are negative, their responses can be harsh. "It was clear to me," the head of a $25 billion firm told us, "that the top executives of one of my largest divisions wanted no part of the new way of doing things at the company. They thought they could simply wait this out." He replaced every one of them within a year.

The consensus of our chief executives was clear. If you decide you want to stay, let the CEO know, proactively and without being sycophantic, that you want to be on the team, and follow up with actions that demonstrate your willingness to go along with the program. This is particularly important when the new leader has won an internal "horse race" and you were previously associated with a different candidate. In such a case, it is imperative to explicitly acknowledge that you accept the board's decision and show a constructive attitude. As the winner of an internal competition at a bank with $100 billion in assets put it, "It would only be normal for a new CEO to be a little suspicious of people from other camps. So you must make a gesture—at least congratulate him—and follow up with action. You would be surprised how few people even do that."

LEAVE YOUR BAGGAGE AT THE DOOR

One CEO of a $3 billion industrial conglomerate offered a list of specific don'ts: "Don't talk about [your compensation], even if you think you were grossly mistreated by the CEO's predecessor. That is not what he wants to deal with yet. Don't talk about your own long-term plans at the company, because your new boss hasn't decided whether you still have a career there yet. Don't raise issues about long-term difficulties you are having with other executives. He does not want to be cornered into choosing one side or the other until he decides what is needed." There will be time for all these things later, he added. "Right now, the CEO will not appreciate your thrusting your own agenda ahead of his, in any form."

Interestingly, our CEOs were adamant that executives should counsel their spouses—of either gender—to be scrupulously politic as well. Anything negative your spouse says is considered to be an unguardedly accurate reflection of your true views; and given the closeness of executive social circles, gossip about your dissatisfaction with the company can easily filter back to the CEO or the board. This, our interviewees agreed, is the kiss of death.

STUDY THE CEO'S WORKING STYLE

Our interviewees also told us that they wanted their direct reports to be sensitive to their working style and then match it. Because it can be difficult to discern your new boss's proclivities simply by observation, it pays to ask about them specifically. One CEO recalled a meeting with a plainspoken executive who company gossips predicted would be an early casualty of the new regime. "He told me he had a reputation for being blunt and then asked how I wanted him to disagree with me," the CEO told us. "I wasn't sure what he meant at first, but he went on to explain: What kind of facts cause me to change my mind—stories from the front line or statistics? Could he disagree in public or only in private? Once he had made his case and failed to convince me, should he try again or just accept that the decision was made? How did I feel about his subordinates or peers knowing he disagreed with something?" By asking intelligent questions about his new boss's working style, the executive prospered throughout the CEO's 12-year tenure.

Moreover, new leaders look for anything that points to potential ethical or behavioral conflicts. If you demonstrate a deaf ear or override the CEO's signals, you can find yourself on the outs. One chief executive fired his head of sales on the basis of such discomfort. "I felt he was just a little sleazy," he told us. "Nothing I could put my finger on, but he somehow made me uncomfortable. I didn't exactly fire him just because of that, but it reduced my tolerance for any other problems. So when another issue came up, I acted right away."

What about contacting your counterpart in the CEO's former company or division in an effort to learn more about his tastes? On this point, our interviewees were split. Some felt that questions about communication style were perfectly fair, and the counterpart might even go further than expected and volunteer extremely valuable information that you didn't ask for. Other CEOs felt that this gambit would be too risky because you don't know anything about the personal relationship between the counterpart and the chief executive—or whether they still talk to each other. One particularly suspicious CEO put it this way: "How do you know that this guy isn't already lobbying for your job?"

UNDERSTAND THE CEO'S AGENDA

According to our chief executives, senior managers could be substantially more effective if they simply took a little time to put themselves in the newcomer's shoes and made an effort to appreciate his or her agenda. First, consider the pressure your new leader is under, especially when it comes to making a strong start. A study of 20 CEOs in 2003 by McKinsey & Company showed that a new chief executive's fate depends heavily on the company's stock performance during his or her first year of tenure. The researchers found that 75% of CEOs whose companies' stock rose during the first 12 months were still in their jobs two years later, but 83% of those whose firms' stock fell were gone by that time. Accordingly, your new boss will be looking for constructive suggestions about actions that he or she can take very quickly. Can you help?

The CEOs we spoke with also pointed out that executives need to confirm their understanding of the new agenda directly with their new boss. While our interviewees understood that their immediate actions sometimes confused their direct reports, they also felt that had the executives made an effort to speak with them about their agendas, the confusion might have been avoided. Even if you've talked to board members about their possible directives for the new CEO, his plans for the company will be influenced by his background, judgments, and expertise, not just the board's disposition. It's important to hear about those ideas directly from him.

PRESENT A REALISTIC AND HONEST GAME PLAN

It's only reasonable for a new CEO to expect you to be prepared to discuss the situation in your division and your plans for progress. Make sure you've thought everything through and then present the facts as clearly as possible. Don't make the mistake of sugarcoating them, however—that would be exactly the wrong approach. A too-rosy report will make your boss ask herself, "Who are you trying to kid?" One CEO who didn't receive straight information from a number of direct reports put it quite bluntly: "I don't have time to sort out trust issues. If you don't show me the negatives, I suspect that either you don't know them or that you will try to hide things from me. If you aren't open with me about problems, I assume you are covering up."

BE ON YOUR "A" GAME

Because your new CEO is on trial, too, it's important to help him or her show positive operating results—and soon. You can't afford to allow your organization to slip into paralysis because of the confusion attending a change at the top. This is no time to rest on your laurels. It's critical to demonstrate that you are active and competent and that important projects are moving full-steam ahead.

One new leader described winnowing the wheat from the chaff this way: "We had lots of interactions, including a four-hour executive meeting once a week. I simply observed who made sure to be there, who was prepared, who was action oriented, who identified solutions versus problems, and who actually followed through on what they said they would do." Based on these impressions, the CEO jettisoned almost half his direct reports within a year and another quarter of the original group in the subsequent six months.

A surprising proportion of our CEOs reported cases of executives who, perhaps assuming that they were invaluable, displayed a dismaying lack of political acumen during the critical "honeymoon" weeks. One leader told of a subordinate who took a two-week vacation during the CEO's first month on the job. "The vacation had been scheduled a long time, and I didn't stop him, but I still never forgave him,"the CEO said. "It was the dumbest thing he could do." Several of our interviewees ranted about troop absences. "Can you believe he was out playing golf with customers half the time in my first six weeks?" one top executive at a $15 billion consumer products firm raged. "He was never there when I tried to reach him. I developed serious questions about his priorities." Certainly, customer entertainment is a norm in many industries, but face time is critical when the new boss is forming impressions.

Another reason to be on top of your game during this period is that your CEO may be too busy to coach you. Perhaps it's unfair, but the reality is that your new boss may not bother to tell you when you make a mistake; make two such errors and you are likely to be shown the door. If you do receive a warning, it may be discernible only from the questions you're asked about operational improvements or results. One new CEO, unsatisfied with the answers he was getting, began asking his head of operations more sharply worded questions over time. The responses did not improve, and the CEO dismissed him six weeks later. When asked if he ever sat the executive down and said, "This is not acceptable work," he laughed and replied, "You know, I guess I didn't. It never occurred to me. I was too busy."

The best way to improve your standing quickly is to take on a project—preferably a special one—in which you must interact extensively with the new leader over a short period of time. All our CEOs agreed on this point. When a third-tier executive in a transportation company did an outstanding job of working with the CEO to reform the firm's customer service interface, for example, the chief executive promoted her to the senior management team. Your new boss will appreciate spending time with you, and if his initial impressions of you have been less than stellar, you might be able to turn his feelings around. No one will ever know whether any early casualties could have been avoided with the right exposure.

OFFER OBJECTIVE OPTIONS

Every new CEO has made difficult trade-offs to protect earnings or to invest in spite of earnings impacts; he has made choices between alternative growth paths and budgeting options. Every interviewee liked the idea of an executive objectively explaining previous budgeting decisions for his department, the rationale behind them, and how the new CEO's priorities might warrant a reassessment of some of those choices. An executive who demonstrates the willingness and ability to constructively engage in a discussion of budgetary options, and helps the CEO translate a new vision into tangible decisions, will be very welcome. Tellingly, not one of the CEOs we spoke with had ever worked with one.

Should you also immediately discuss major strategy changes with your new boss? The answer is, "It depends." One CEO thought it would be helpful to hear an unbiased assessment of the division's prospects and receive a thoughtful range of options that he or she might consider. Others appreciated the sentiment, but felt that a new CEO would not yet be ready to assess strategic issues. Regardless of how or when you choose to discuss the alternatives, it is important not to appear self-serving; if you try to persuade the CEO to quickly invest huge amounts in your business, don't expect a warm reception. "I want real choices," one CEO said, "not end runs around the collective judgment of the other executives."

CEO changes are stressful for all senior executives. The danger of being pushed out is real, and the difficulty of landing on your feet is severe. On the other hand, opportunities are real, too. Many executives have reinvigorated their careers within a company after a change at the top; others have found fulfillment away from the corporate world.

Of course, whether or not you follow the advice of our interviewees is entirely up to you. The former CEO of one of the largest financial institutions in the country perhaps put it best when he said, "Make your personal decision about whether the new guy's style, vision, and business practices are ones you want to live with. Then commit or get out. Otherwise, everyone's life will be hell. And the result will be the same anyway."

About the Research

IN EARLY 2006, using the most recent data available, we assembled a database comprising executives who were included in the 2002, 2003, and 2004 proxy statements of the top 1,000 companies (as determined by market cap) in the United States. There were, on average, four executives per organization, excluding the CEO. By comparing the companies' statements from year to year, we were able to learn what effects a change of top leadership in either 2002 or 2003 had on those executives.

We also created a database of changes among all those listed generally as "executive officers" (about ten per company) in the annual reports of a large sample of those firms during the same time period. This allowed us to look at the impact of CEO changes on a larger group of executives.

Next, we used Hoover's to determine the most recently reported employment status of the executives in our sample who had left their companies after a new CEO arrived. This gave us a wealth of statistical information about the aftermath of a shift in top leadership.

To confirm that the results in our sample years were indicative of longer trends, we cross-checked them with earlier academic work on management turnover. Our findings were remarkably consistent in both direction and degree.

We felt that practical advice would enrich our interpretation of the data, so we extensively interviewed more than a dozen professional CEOs who had taken over at least one very large, usually public, company. They represented a broad cross-section of industries, from high tech to financial services to consumer goods, and a wide range of sizes—from several hundred million dollars in sales to more than $25 billion.

Originally published in May 2007
Reprint R0705C

Ending the CEO Succession Crisis

RAM CHARAN

Executive Summary

THE CEO SUCCESSION process is broken. Many companies have no meaningful succession plans, and few of the ones that do are happy with them. CEO tenure is shrinking; in fact, two out of five CEOs fail in their first 18 months.

It isn't just that more CEOs are being replaced; it's that they're being replaced *badly*. The problems extend to every aspect of CEO succession: internal development programs, board supervision, and outside recruitment.

While many organizations do a decent job of nurturing middle managers, few have set up the comprehensive programs needed to find the half-dozen true CEO candidates out of the thousands of leaders in their midst. Even more damaging is the failure of boards to devote enough attention to

125

succession. Search committee members often have no experience hiring CEOs; lacking guidance, they supply either the narrowest or the most general of requirements and then fail to vet either the candidates or the recruiters.

The result is that too often new CEOs are plucked from the well-worn Rolodexes of a remarkably small number of recruiters. These candidates may be strong in charisma but may lack critical skills or otherwise be a bad fit with the company. The resulting high turnover is particularly damaging, since outside CEOs often bring in their own teams, can cause the company to lose focus, and are especially costly to be rid of.

Drawing on over 35 years of experience with CEO succession, the author explains how companies can create a deep pool of internal candidates, how boards can consistently align strategy and leadership development, and how directors can get their money's worth from recruiters. Choosing a CEO should be not one decision but an amalgam of thousands of decisions made by many people every day over years.

W E TALK ABOUT LEADERSHIP as though leaders—like Tolstoy's happy families—are all alike. But CEO leadership should be a subject apart because it is unique in scope and substance and of incomparable importance. CEOs' performance determines the fates of corporations, which collectively influence whole economies. Our standard of living depends upon excellence at the very top.

Who, then, would dispute that CEO selection deserves perpetual front-burner attention from the custodians of a company's welfare? Surely, when time or trauma ushers in change, organizations should be ready with a clear view of current and future needs and with carefully tended pools of candidates.

But they're not. The CEO succession process is broken in North America and is no better in many other parts of the world. Almost half of companies with revenue greater than $500 million have no meaningful CEO succession plan, according to the National Association of Corporate Directors. Even those that have plans aren't happy with them. The Corporate Leadership Council (CLC), a human-resource research organization, surveyed 276 large companies last year and found that only 20% of responding HR executives were satisfied with their top-management succession processes.

That deficiency is simply inexcusable. A CEO or board that has been in place for six or seven years and has not yet provided a pool of qualified candidates, and a robust process for selecting the next leader, is a failure. Everyone talks about emulating such best practitioners as General Electric, but few work very hard at it.

The result of poor succession planning is often poor performance, which translates into higher turnover and corporate instability. As increased transparency, more vocal institutional investors, and more active boards make greater demands, CEO tenures continue to shrink. Booz Allen Hamilton reports that the global average is now just 7.6 years, down from 9.5 years in 1995. And two out of every five new CEOs fail in the first 18 months, as Dan Ciampa cites in his article "Almost Ready" in last month's HBR.

The problem isn't just that more CEOs are being replaced. The problem is that, in many cases, CEOs are being replaced *badly*. Too often, new leaders are plucked from the well-worn Rolodexes of a small recruiting oligarchy and appointed by directors who have little experience hiring anyone for a position higher than COO, vice chairman, CFO, or president of a large business unit. Hiring a CEO is simply different.

Coaxing former leaders out of retirement is another popular way to fill the void. Celebrated examples include Harry Stonecipher at Boeing, Bill Stavropoulos of Dow Chemical, and Jamie Houghton at Corning. But most "boomerang CEOs" return for just a couple of years, long enough to restore credibility and put a real succession candidate in place. They are not the long-term solution.

To increase their chances of finding a leader who will serve long and well, companies must do three things. First, they should have available a deep pool of internal candidates kept well stocked by a leadership development process that reaches from the bottom to the top. Second, boards should create, then continually update and refine, a succession plan and have in place a thoughtful process for making decisions about candidates. Finally, directors considering outside candidates should be exacting, informed drivers of the executive search process, leading recruiters rather than being led by them.

In my 35 years advising corporations, I have participated in dozens of CEO selections and have closely monitored numerous executive pipelines. Drawing on that experience, I will in these pages first explain why companies make poor appointments and then suggest what they can instead do to make good ones. Using these guidelines, organizations can ensure that all participants—directors, executive recruiters, and sitting CEOs—perform wisely and appropriately when it comes time to choose their next leader.

The Trouble with Outsiders

When companies lack the culture or the processes to grow their own heirs apparent, they have no choice but to look outside. More than a third (37%) of the *Fortune* 1,000 companies are run by external recruits, according to the public affairs firm Burson-Marsteller. Although global data are harder to come by, the worldwide trend appears to be similar. But external candidates are in most cases a greater risk because directors and top management cannot know them as well as they know their own people.

Outsiders are generally chosen because they can do *a* job—turn around the company or restructure the portfolio. But *the* job is to lead a hugely complex organization over many years through an unpredictable progression of shifting markets and competitive terrains. Unfortunately, the requirements for that larger job are often not well defined by the board, which may be focused on finding a savior.

The results are not surprising. In North America, 55% of outside CEOs who departed in 2003 were forced to resign by their boards, compared with 34% of insiders, Booz Allen reports. In Europe, 70% of departing outsiders got the boot, compared with 55% of insiders. Some outside CEOs are barely around long enough to see their photographs hung in the headquarters lobby. Gil Amelio left Apple 17 months after he arrived from National Semiconductor. Ex-IBMer Richard Thoman was out of the top spot at Xerox after 13 months. David Siegel gave

up the wheel at Avis Rent A Car for US Airways but
departed two years later.

Even under the best circumstances, CEO selection is
something of a batting average: Companies will not hit
successfully every time. But two or more consecutive
outsider outs can have a devastating effect on employees,
partners, and strategic position. New leaders import new
teams and management styles. Continuity and momen-
tum collapse, the energy to execute dwindles, and morale
plummets as employees obsess about who will get the
next pink slip. Rather than focus on the competition,
companies starts to look inward. Bad external appointments are also expensive, since even poor performance
is rewarded with rich severance packages.

The Trouble with Insiders

On the other hand, sometimes an external candidate
exists who is, very simply, the best available choice. A
skillful, diligent board may discover an outstanding fit
between an outsider and the job at hand. Lou Gerstner
and IBM spring to mind. And boards must remember
that just as outsiders are not uniformly bad choices,
insiders are not uniformly good ones. In certain situations,
internal candidates actually present the greater risk.

Some concerns about insiders, ironically, emerge from
their very closeness to the company. For example, as
"known quantities," they may sail through a lax due-
diligence process. Or their social networks and psycho-
logical ties may complicate efforts to change the culture.
Some will not have had the right experience or been
tested in the right ways. Individuals from functional
areas may not be up to the task of leading the entire
business. Or a shift in the industry or market landscape

may render carefully nurtured skills irrelevant. In some cases, the credibility of the outgoing CEO or management team may be so sullied that only a new broom can sweep the company clean.

What's more, companies that have no ongoing senior management development program (currently more the rule than the exception) will in all probability need to look outside, maybe for as long as the next ten to 20 years. Outside candidates, in other words, should always be an option. But so long as they remain the only option, and boards lack rigor in identifying and assessing them, succession is imperiled.

The Trouble with CEO Development

Many organizations do a decent job nurturing middle managers, but meaningful leadership development stops well below the apex. The problem manifests itself as a dearth of senior managers, for which companies must increasingly shop in other neighborhoods. Almost half of respondents to the CLC survey had hired a third or more of their senior executive teams from outside, but only 22% of those did so because they considered external candidates irresistibly appealing. Rather, 45% of all respondents judged that it would take too long or be too expensive to develop successors internally.

It's easy to understand why they feel that way. Even where strong development programs exist, very few leaders will ever be qualified to run the company. *Very few.* A $25 billion corporation with 70,000 employees, for instance, may have 3,000 leaders, perhaps 50 to 100 of whom would qualify for one of the ten jobs just below the top. That same company would be fortunate to field five strong internal candidates for CEO—and two or

three is a more realistic number. General Electric had
around 225,000 workers in 1993 when Jack Welch
identified 20 potential successors; over seven years,
he winnowed the number to three. In CEO succession,
it takes a ton of ore to produce an ounce of gold.

Furthermore, the window in which to spot CEO talent
is narrow. Companies require sufficiently seasoned candidates who can be counted on to hold the top job for
ten years or more. That puts the age of accession at
between 46 and 52. In my experience, for a candidate to
be ready by 46, serious development should start by age
30. Recognizing which five saplings in a 3,000-tree forest
are the ones to nurture requires a degree of discernment
that most line managers and HR departments lack and
few are developing.

Some companies do identify candidates early but then
fail to evaluate them properly. Such organizations often
turn evaluation over to HR, which may rely excessively
on packaged databases of leadership traits developed by
researchers in the human behavior field. Those programs
compare internal high potentials with generic benchmarks along many dimensions, a process that creates
fragmented profiles of some cookie-cutter ideal rather
than nuanced, individualized portraits. What's more,
most of those dimensions reflect only the personality
traits and not the skills required of a CEO.

Nor do many companies properly nurture the candidates they identify. Some misjudge the business's needs
and consequently emphasize the wrong talents. Only
24% of organizations the CLC surveyed believe their
leadership development efforts are aligned with their
strategic goals. And those goals can be a moving target,
changing in response to sometimes tectonic shifts in
the external environment. The marketplace changes.

Technology changes. Employees' skills become obsolete even as they develop. What's more, very few in-house executive education programs are designed to impart the skills and know-how that a CEO needs.

But the larger issue is that true development happens on the job, not in a classroom. Few companies know how to get their best people the experiences that would prepare them for the CEO role or to rigorously evaluate them in the jobs they do perform. Many companies, for example, still equate leadership development with circulating candidates through multiple functions. In the 1970s, that was the rule at AT&T, IBM, and Xerox, companies that produced leaders who went on to become CEOs elsewhere—and in some cases failed.

The problem with that approach is that potential candidates don't stay long enough in one position to live with the consequences of their decisions. In addition, functional leaders learn to lead functions, not whole companies. Faced with external competition, they fall back on their functional expertise. You can mine all possible lessons from a turn as VP of marketing and still be blindsided by a P&L.

The Trouble with Boards

Bob Stemple's short stint as the head of General Motors ended ingloriously in 1992—and so did the accepted wisdom that boards should automatically bless the departing CEO's handpicked successor.

Yet while directors describe CEO succession as one of their most consuming issues, they don't appear consumed by it. In a survey by Mercer Delta and the University of Southern California, 40% of corporate directors called their involvement in CEO succession planning less than optimal. (I would hazard to add that far fewer are satisfied with the *outcome* of their involvement.) Only 21% responded that they were satisfied with their level of participation in developing internal candidates for senior management.

A packed agenda is the chief culprit: Governance and fiduciary duties, in particular, command an outsize share of boards' attention. Mercer Delta asked directors to compare the amount of time they spend now with the amount they spent a year earlier on nine key activities. Large majorities reported devoting more or many more hours to monitoring accounting, Sarbanes-Oxley, risk, and financial performance. They also reported spending less time interacting with and preparing potential CEO successors than on any other activity. Yet boards' work on succession represents probably 80% of the value they deliver. If the choice of CEO successor is superb, all subsequent decisions become easier.

Another huge problem is that the vast majority of search committee members have had no experience working together on a CEO succession. As a result, they seldom coalesce into deep-delving bodies that get to the pith of their companies' fundamental needs. So they end up approaching their search with only the demands of the moment or—worse—the broadest of requirements.

As they audition candidates, directors may be seduced by reputation, particularly if they're considering a Wall Street or media darling. A few aspiring CEOs employ publicists who flog rosy stories to journalists; when those leaders are up for other jobs, their press-bestowed halos follow them. Board members can also be blinded by charisma, by the sheer leaderishness of a candidate. There is nothing intrinsically wrong with charisma, though some criticize it as the sheep's clothing in which hubris lurks. But too often directors become so focused on what candidates are *like* that they don't press hard enough to discover what candidates can and cannot *do*.

For example, one board looking for a new CEO after firing the old one asked for someone who could build a great team and get things done. The recruiter presented such a person—an energetic, focused candidate whose personal qualities quickly won over directors. What the organization really needed was someone who could create a stream of new products and win shelf space from powerful retailers in a volatile marketplace. Unfortunately, the directors never specified those requirements or raised them either during interviews or the background check.

The candidate's upstream-marketing skills were poor to nonexistent. The company's market share declined precipitously, and three years later the CEO was out on his ear. On its second try, the board concentrated so hard on marketing that it ignored execution. The next CEO was a visionary and a marketing genius but was unable to get things done. The company, once first in its market, will probably be sold or stumble into Chapter 11.

Finally, directors too often shunt due diligence onto recruiters. As a result, that process can be quite superficial. One company that left vetting to its recruiter and its investment banker found itself saddled with a leader who botched critical people issues. At a postmortem three years later, directors discovered that at his former company the CEO had routinely punted people problems to the chairman, who had been CEO before him and occupied the office next to his. That would have been nice to know before the pen touched the contract.

The Trouble with Recruiters

Executive recruiters are honest and highly professional. Still, they can wield disproportionate influence in CEO succession decisions. One reason is concentration. Just three recruiters control some 80% of the *Fortune* 100 CEO search market (a single firm claims fully 60% of it), and one or two people within those companies direct the most important searches. These firms' social networks are vast and powerful. Anyone with a smidgen of ambition in the corporate world knows whom they have to know to get ahead.

At the same time, board members' inexperience and consequent inability to precisely define their needs makes recruiters' task difficult. Recruiters must satisfy their clients yet also manage them, helping the search committee to gel so they can extract the criteria they need while keeping requirements broad enough to cast the widest talent net possible.

When committees don't gel, recruiters may step into the vacuum with their own criteria, and directors too often let them. Unfortunately, no executive recruiter can grasp the subtleties of a client's business as well as the client can. In the absence of effective direction, recruiters generally approach each search with a boilerplate of the 20 or so attributes they consider most desirable for any CEO. That formula tends to overemphasize generic qualities like character and vision, as well as team-building, change-management, and relationship skills. Psychology and chemistry are also very important to executive recruiters: Like directors, they may let a personality surplus overshadow a skills deficit.

In one—granted, extreme—case, the longtime CEO of a company with four highly successful businesses and a huge debt level was retiring. The recruiter produced a list of six candidates, pressing one—the head of a very large division at a multinational company—hard on the board. Yet all the recruiter gave the directors was a page-and-a-half description of this candidate's leadership skills; a list of his extensive connections with unions, customers, and government bodies; and an outline of his swift rise through the organization.

A financial performance history for the candidate's division was not included and not publicly available, so a member of the search committee began to dig. He discovered that return on assets under the candidate's supervision was miniscule over the previous five years, even though his division was four times larger than the entire company considering him for CEO. Furthermore, this man had never earned cost of capital in his life. Even so, the recruiter wanted to put him in charge of a business that had certainly done so—and that hoped to rise to the next level.

Fortunately, after much debate, the committee vetoed the recommendation, opting instead for number three on the recruiter's list— the president of another company, who had consistently improved performance and delivered a 20% return on equity. In his first three years, this new CEO took the stock from 24 to 108 in a slow-moving industry. The board was happy. Management was happy. The recruiter's preferred candidate was happy when he was placed at another, larger company—but then he was fired in six months.

Executive recruiters also succumb to the usual-suspects bias, primarily looking for new heads above other companies' necks. It is just plain easier to compile a list of sitting CEOs than to make a case for—or take a risk on—a COO or an executive VP. Some recruiters go so far as to approach sitting CEOs, even with no specific jobs to dangle, and urge them to consider looking elsewhere. The recruiters' goal is to loosen a prized gem from its setting and thereby beat a fellow recruiter to the punch.

Sometimes, the board's selection of recruiter is flawed from the start. A director may jump the gun, recommending a recruiter he has worked well with even before the search committee is formed. Nor do most boards examine search firms' track records—that is, how many of the CEOs the firm has placed have succeeded and how many have failed. Even if directors did ask that question, they're not likely to get the answer because it appears no one is monitoring recruiters' performance. The stock-buying public, by contrast, knows exactly how well directors score on their CEO choices.

How to Succeed at Succession

Charlie Bell's ascension to the top spot at McDonald's within hours of Jim Cantalupo's death reflected well on a company that had its house in order, particularly when compared—as it inevitably was—with Coca-Cola's simultaneous travails. Similarly, NBC's early, orderly announcement that Brian Williams would replace network news anchor Tom Brokaw stands in stark relief to CBS's public uncertainty over Dan Rather's successor. (Anchors are not CEOs, of course, but they are even more visible and arguably as consequential to their organizations' fortunes.)

By now it should be clear that the most important thing companies can do to improve succession is to bolster their leadership development and focus on those very rare people in their ranks who might one day be CEO.

Organizations must identify high-potential candidates early in their careers, and global companies must look in all the countries where they operate. As candidates enter the development pipeline, managers must constantly align their charges' education and on-the-job experience with the emerging landscape. And they must rigorously assess the candidates' performance at each developmental stage.

The very best preparation for CEOs is progression through positions with responsibility for steadily larger and more complex P&L centers. A candidate might start by managing a single product, then a customer segment, then a country, then several product lines, then a business unit, and then a division. Whatever the progression, P&L responsibility at every level is key. The Thomson Corporation, a global provider of information solutions, comprises more than 100 P&Ls, so its top people have abundant opportunity to run a $50 million to $100 million business. "That's the best crucible for formulating leaders that I know of," says Jim Smith, executive vice president of human resources and administration.

Companies not set up to provide such opportunities should create jobs—large projects or small internal organizations—that exercise the P&L muscle. Otherwise, they risk elevating an internal candidate who is not prepared. For example, one $10 billion company in a highly capital-intensive and unionized industry has targeted as CEO successor the head of its smallest division. The candidate is a brilliant, articulate young man but has no experience running a big business in general or this type of business in particular (his own division is knowledge intensive, and unionized labor has no presence). The board is considering creating a deputy position within its largest division for this person and making the 59-year-old current division head (who will retire in three years) his coach, granting that coach a bonus if he ensures his successor's success.

Companies with inflexible functional structures will probably be forced to import P&L-tested leaders from outside and place them in very high positions. To reduce the risk, they should bring in such executives three or four years before the expected succession. That can be challenging, however, because many will demand appointment to the top spot in less than a year.

But leadership development is just part of the solution. Boards, too, can greatly improve the chances of finding a strong successor by acting vigilantly before and during the search. Senior executive development should be overseen by the board's compensation and organization committee, which needs to receive periodic reports on the entire pool of potential CEOs and regular updates on those bobbing near the top of it. The committee should spend a third of its time examining lists of the top 20 candidates in the leadership pipeline. In addition, at least 15% of the 60 or so hours that members meet as a full board should be devoted to succession. At minimum, the board ought to dedicate two sessions a year to hashing over at least five CEO candidates, both internal and external.

And directors should personally get to know the company's rising stars. Promising leaders should be invited to board meetings and to the dinners that precede board meetings, and members should talk with them informally whenever possible. Directors should also meet with and observe candidates within the natural habitats of their business operations. In this way, when it comes time to single out CEO candidates, directors will be considering a set of very well-known quantities.

The "Fit" Imperative

The goal of all these interactions and deliberations is for board members to reach a highly refined but dynamic understanding of the CEO position and their options for it long before appointing a successor. Company leaders should be as well defined as puzzle pieces; their strengths and experiences must match the shape of their organizations' needs. That is, they simply must *fit*. Boards achieve fit by specifying, in terms as precise as possible, three or four aspects of talent, know-how, and experience that are nonnegotiable.

Ideally, these attributes pertain to the organization's dominant needs for the next several years, but they should also relate to future growth. In one recent CEO succession, the company, in conjunction with a boutique recruiting firm, began with impossibly broad criteria that included everything from industry leader to change agent. The process floundered until the search committee narrowed its focus to three qualities: experience in segmenting markets according to customer needs; the talent to grow the business organically; and a track record of building strong executive teams. Those three skills, in addition to general leadership traits, delineated the pond in which this company fished.

The job of defining such qualities belongs to the search committee, which should form well before succession is scheduled to take place. As they wrestle with requirements, committee members must constantly keep in mind the company's changing circumstances, so that an understanding of what currently works doesn't congeal into what works, period.

For example, Bank of America flourished under deal maker par excellence Hugh McColl, Jr., for years. But by the time he stepped down in 2001, integration, rather than acquisition, had become the dominant challenge. Having recognized the altered environment several years before, BOA's board chose not a leader in McColl's image but instead Ken Lewis, a company veteran proficient at integration of acquisitions and organic growth. (For an example of how a company integrates its leadership development with its strategy, see the sidebar "The Living Succession Tree.")

Specific, nonnegotiable criteria also let directors keep control when they work with executive recruiters. With good direction, search firms can be a valuable source of objectivity—benchmarking internal candidates against outsiders and making sure that board members consider all possibilities, even if they prefer an insider. Some companies even bring in recruiters to do independent assessments of insider candidates. Their concurrence with a board's judgment carries weight with shareholders and potential critics.

Search firms ask boards to recommend candidates, and they take those recommendations seriously. But, ultimately, it is the recruiter who compiles the list, and the compiler of the list wields considerable influence. Directors must require from recruiters detailed explanations of how the candidates fulfill their criteria. A ten-page report on each is reasonable.

When the time comes to select the new CEO, directors—ordinarily a polite breed, unaccustomed to challenging one another or asking discomforting questions—must engage in a vigorous discussion of the candidates' comparative merits. One search committee that did an outstanding job making the final decision invited five candidates (two internal and three external) to a hotel for a couple of days. The two internal candidates were favorites of two different directors. On the first day, the committee interviewed three candidates, two external and one internal. The directors split into two groups of three, and each group spoke with one candidate for 90 minutes. After these interviews, the directors broke for 45 minutes to share impressions, then switched candidates. Then the two groups of directors took turns interviewing the third candidate, similarly sharing impressions informally. At the end of the first day, the committee members debated over dinner, and the director who had originally advocated for the internal candidate volunteered that he was indeed not the strongest choice. The next day, they repeated the process with the two other candidates, and the results were remarkably the same, with the director who had originally advocated for the internal candidate changing his mind. In the course of these discussions, all hidden agendas fell away, requirements were honed, and directors were able to reach consensus.

Finally, board members must do due diligence on outside candidates—and do it well. Directors must seek reliable external sources and demand candor from them. Board members should ask first about the candidate's natural talents. If those gifts—admirable as they may be—do not match the position's specific profile, that candidate is not worth pursuing. Needless to say, due diligence is also the time to root out any fatal character flaws.

At this point, the role of the outgoing CEO is chiefly consultative. He or she must be active in spotting and grooming talent, help define the job's requirements, provide accurate information about both internal and external candidates, and facilitate discussions between candidates and directors. But when the choice of successor is imminent, make no mistake: That decision belongs to the board.

Inside a Development Engine

Despite the current crisis, we know it is possible to build organizations that reliably produce great CEOs. Starting after World War II, a few corporations emerged as veritable leadership factories. Companies like General Electric, Emerson Electric, Sherwin-Williams, Procter & Gamble, and Johnson & Johnson managed to stock not only their own corner offices but also many others. (Of course even great companies sometimes stumble: Procter & Gamble had a failure from within when it promoted Durk Jager to the top spot. But it is going great guns under the stewardship of company veteran A.G. Lafley.)

Reuben Mark has sat atop Colgate-Palmolive for 20 years, so the company's CEO succession chops have not been recently proven. But I believe the consumer products giant has a first-rate process for identifying and developing CEO talent. At the very least it produced three internal candidates who are excellent prospects for the job.

Colgate-Palmolive does business in more than 200 countries, and its emerging leaders are correspondingly international and diverse. Leadership evaluation begins during the first year of employment. "It may seem strange to talk about someone who's been here just a year when discussing the pipeline to the CEO," says Bob Joy, senior vice president of global human resources. "But the earlier you start to identify talent, the earlier you can provide the job assignments and develop the broad business experience needed by a CEO candidate."

Each subsidiary identifies its own high potentials and submits that list to local general managers, who add and subtract names and then hand the list off to the division heads. These lists wend their way up the chain until they reach the Colgate-Palmolive Human Resource (CPHR) committee, composed of Colgate's CEO, president, COO, the senior VP of HR, and the senior candidates up for the top job. CPHR modifies and consolidates the lists into a single master list, dispatching it back down the ranks where managers can contest decisions made by those above them. The process takes place once a year.

Those who make the cut are deployed in one of three tracks. The first track, local talent, is for relatively junior staff who might become the direct reports of a general manager. Someone more advanced would be designated regional talent, and given, for example, a significant position in Asia. The most elevated track—global talent—is the reservoir from which the most senior jobs are filled.

Throughout their careers, all these high potentials receive assignments that stretch their abilities and expand their knowledge, exposing them to a variety of markets, cultures, consumers, and business circumstances. CPHR itself designs career paths for general managers and higher positions because the committee is at the same time dynamically developing the profile of Colgate's future leadership team. (Also, says Joy, "you can imagine the kind of resistance you'd get from a division president who would like to keep his high-potential people in his own area.") The thousand or so highest high potentials (out of a total pool of about 2,000) receive outside executive coaching, which includes 360-degree feedback on current and past assignments.

Having identified its high potentials, Colgate strives to bolster their connection to the company. One tactic is recognition: "If you're talking about the future leaders of your company, you want them to feel special," says Joy. "You want them to have Colgate in their veins." Toward that end, the company sponsors a series of "visibility programs." One, for example, gathers high potentials from all over the world at Colgate's New York headquarters for weeklong sessions during which they meet with every senior leader in the company. In addition, each high potential receives a special stock grant, which arrives with a personal letter from the CEO.

Colgate's global growth program mandates that all senior managers retain 90% of their high potentials or lose some compensation. If a high potential at any level, anywhere in the world, does resign, the CEO, the COO, the president, and Joy are alerted within 24 hours and move immediately to retain that person.

Perhaps most important, Joy collaborates with the office of the chairman to connect directors early and often with high potentials in all areas. At the most senior level, functional leaders introduce the board to the top two or three most-promising heirs for their own positions, adding detailed analyses of those candidates' strengths and weaknesses. Emerging leaders routinely take part in presentations to the board and meet informally with directors over lunch. Board members closely track the progress not of one or two people but of the top 200, frequently discussing how each piece fits into the puzzle and what experiences or skills might improve that fit.

As a result, when CEO succession looms, the board and top management will be able to select from candidates they have spent many, many years observing and evaluating. "If you start five years or even ten years before the CEO is going to retire," says Joy, "it may be too late."

Of course Colgate-Palmolive—like General Electric— tackles succession from a position of strength. Its CEO has been two decades in the saddle, and he is passionate on the subject of an heir. Companies with less-veteran chiefs—and whose boards have been negligent in this area—will probably need to line up candidates quickly, while laying a deeper pipeline. They will in all likelihood have to bring in outsiders and position them to gain the requisite business and industry experience. That may mean shaking up the leadership team and reporting structures to free up slots in which outsiders can be tested. This restructuring will probably be resented, but it is necessary pain.

A quick infusion of talent may be a company's only course, but it is no way to run a railroad. Organizations without meaningful pipelines must start now to put them in place. Young companies should create the processes that will come to fruition in five or ten years' time. Choosing the CEO's successor is not one decision but the amalgam of thousands of decisions made by many people every day over years and years. Such meticulous, steady attention to defining needs and evaluating candidates produces strong leaders and inspires succession planners at lower levels to exercise the same discipline.

The trend of CEO failures must be reversed. CEO succession is all boards' paramount responsibility; nothing else so profoundly affects their companies' futures. Directors must start investing their time and energy today. The call for a new leader could come tomorrow.

The Secret of Session C

LOTS OF PEOPLE KNOW ABOUT SESSION C, General Electric's annual, dialogue-intensive review of how its leadership resources match up with its business direction. But inside Session C is a process that almost no one knows about. It's called "tandem assessment," and it is among GE's most potent tools for evaluating CEO candidates—and for helping those rising stars evaluate themselves.

Every year, GE selects a different set of 20 to 25 leaders who might grow into CEOs or top functional leaders and sits each one down for a three- to four-hour session with two human resource heads from outside the person's own business unit. The HR executives trace the budding leader's progression from early childhood (where he grew up, how his parents influenced his style of thinking, what his early values were) through recent accomplishments. They then conduct an exhaustive fact-finding mission both inside and outside the organization, including 360-degree reviews, massive reference checks, and interviews with bosses, direct reports, customers, and peers. Largely eschewing psychology, tandem assessment concentrates instead on observed, measurable performance within the business.

The product of all this effort is a 15- to 20-page document that charts the high potential's work and development over decades. The report—brimming with accolades but also detailing areas for improvement—goes to the nascent leader, who uses it to improve his or her game. It also goes to the individual's business head, the senior human-resource executive in the person's unit, and to corporate headquarters, where it is avidly perused by GE's chairman, the three vice chairmen, and Bill Conaty, senior vice president for corporate human resources. "I usually wait until the end of the workday to read one of these because it takes an hour or so," says Conaty. "You find out incredibly interesting things about people in this process."

Tandem assessment is so intensive that only those swimming closest to the C-suite headwaters undergo it. But GE also encourages business units to conduct their own miniversions of the exercise.

The process not only hands rising leaders a mirror but also broadens their support network. Using HR executives from outside the subject's business unit ensures objectivity and gives the promising star two new mentors and two new reality checks. "If something pops up during your career that doesn't feel quite right and you want outside calibration," Conaty explains, "you might call one of these individuals and say, 'Hey, look, everybody is telling me great things here, but this just happened. Would you read anything into it?'"

The Living Succession Tree

FOUR YEARS AGO, top management at the Thomson Corporation realized that its CEO succession process had passed out of life and into a stagnant existence on paper. Leadership development chugged along separately from business planning.

Human resource groups produced reams of documents and charts dense with the branches of succession trees. "We never used them," says Jim Smith, executive vice president of human resources and administration at the $7 billion global company. "I never saw anybody go to a chart and say, 'Let's look at this.'"

So the company decided to rethink talent management in order to field leaders who could run Thomson under whatever conditions might exist. The new process is built on two principles: Succession planning should happen in lockstep with strategy making, and the current CEO should be intimately and visibly involved.

Each February, Thomson's 200 top managers gather to review corporate initiatives. Then in April, CEO Richard Harrington, CEO Robert Daleo, and Smith conduct strategy reviews with emerging leaders in every business unit. Goals coming out of those talks—related to markets, customers, products, and growth areas—accompany the trio into the next round of discussions, which takes place in June and focuses on management development.

At that point, Harrington, Daleo, and Smith devote eight full days to listening to senior executives (including CEO candidates) report on *their* highest potentials. The trio insists on concrete examples throughout. "It's so easy to generalize on how somebody's doing: 'He's a good guy' and 'She's terrific with people,'" says Smith. "We want to pin down the facts beneath that. 'You say she's good with people. Give me some examples of who she's developed. How many have been promoted?'"

The same people who attended the strategy meetings attend the leadership development meetings, so everyone in the room understands what talent the business requires. And when those same people reconvene again a few months later to discuss budgets, conclusions from the strategy and leadership development rounds inform their decisions. By year's end, Thomson has tightly integrated strategy, leadership, and budget plans. And Harrington and his senior team have spent many, many hours getting to know the company's most-promising CEO candidates.

Smith has three recommendations for companies interested in crafting a similar system, which has proved constructive to managers and the board alike. First, make sure the CEO devotes considerable personal time to identifying, getting to know, and developing leaders. Second, treat leadership development as part of the process used to run the business. And finally, make the process informal enough to encourage conversation. "We used to produce books," says Smith. "Now we have conversations."

Originally published in February 2005
Reprint R0502C

Solve the Succession Crisis by Growing Inside-Outside Leaders

JOSEPH L. BOWER

Executive Summary

IN HIS ANALYSIS OF 1,800 successions, Harvard Business School professor Bower found that companies performed significantly better when they appointed insiders to the job of CEO. Other researchers, including Jim Collins in *Good to Great,* have come to similar conclusions working from different data sets. Yet Bower finds far too many companies have no succession plans; as a result, when the time comes to name a new chief executive, more firms turn to outsiders.

Both insider and outsider CEOs have strengths and weaknesses at the start. Insiders know the company and its people but are often blind to the need for radical change. Outsiders see the need for a new approach but can't make the necessary changes because they don't know the organization or industry sector well enough. What companies must do, then, is find a way to nurture what Bower calls *inside-outsiders*—internal candidates who have outside perspective.

Often such executives have spent much of their time away from the mainstream of the organization, and away from headquarters, living with now opportunities and threats. Before becoming CEO, Procter & Gamble's A.G. Lafley, for instance, worked for years building P&G's Chinese cosmetics operation rather than the core detergent business. IBM's Sam Palmisano was a champion of software and open systems at a time when Big Blue was essentially a closed-system, hardware-oriented company.

Nascent inside-outsiders should enter the CEO-training process by the time they are 30 and be given the opportunity to manage a whole business, so that they become good insiders. But they also need to be mentored with an eye toward preserving their outsider perspective, so they learn how to turn their new ideas into great businesses and are protected from old-timers who might be inclined to teach them a lesson.

I WAS APPALLED TO LEARN recently that 60% of the respondents to a poll of 1,380 HR directors of large U.S. companies said their firms have no CEO succession plans in place. As this finding suggests, too many companies have over the past two decades ignored the hard work of building future leaders while senior executives have focused increasingly on meeting the next quarter's earnings target. When the time comes to name a new CEO, more firms look outside. Yet strong evidence supports the notion that a well-groomed insider is a key to sustained company performance. In my analysis of 1,800 successions, for instance, I found that company performance was significantly better when insiders succeeded to the job of CEO. Other researchers, including Jim Collins in *Good to Great,* have come to similar conclusions working from different data sets.

Such quantitative research on CEO succession confirms but does not explain why more outsiders are being hired, why qualified insider leadership correlates with better company performance, or what relationship exists between those two trends. These ambiguities have prompted me to consider what I could add to the data-centered research from a qualitative review of a decade of my own and others' case studies and interviews, as well as from my experience managing successions as an outside director. That review made one thing unambiguously clear to me: A critical difference between companies that manage succession well and those that don't is the understanding that succession is a process, not an event. The process begins years before the event. Something else was clear: Both insider and outsider CEOs have strengths and weaknesses when they begin. Insiders know the company and its people but are often blind to the need for radical change—they've drunk the Kool-Aid. Outsiders see the need for a new approach but can't foster change because they don't know the company or industry sector well enough. What organizations need, then, is to find a way to nurture what I call *inside-outsiders*—that is, internal candidates who have outside perspective. For some companies, that may look like mission impossible. But the succession crisis will only get worse if companies don't tackle the problem.

The CEO Does Matter

Recently, there's been a reaction against focusing too much on the CEO—with some justification. Top teams, as much as CEOs themselves, are crucial to the execution of a great strategy. Nonetheless, strong CEOs are worth studying. They wield enormous power. And as stewards of the corporate purpose, their ability to make sense of the business environment and to craft and articulate the mission and the strategy are central to long-term success.

Nothing illustrates the point better than the last 35 years of succession at General Electric. Reginald Jones took the helm at GE in 1972. He developed the strategic-planning system he inherited from his predecessors into the model for companies everywhere. He made huge changes in GE's portfolio, exiting the computer business and acquiring the giant inflation hedge, Utah International. Jones's GE regularly outperformed the U.S. GDP by more than 25%. Recognizing the dawn of a very different environment in 1981, successor Jack Welch proceeded in two or three years to dismantle much of the planning and organizational structure Jones had put in place. Welch sold Utah, acquired RCA, and built a huge financial services business. Entire levels of middle management and staff disappeared. In the second decade of his tenure, GE's market capitalization grew more than 1,000%. Welch's successor, Jeff Immelt, is changing GE once again. He is making major investments in biosciences, water, security, and platforms for infrastructure growth in emerging countries. The stock market is giving him the same cool reception it gave Welch in his first decade, but GE is growing both revenues and profits as it changes.

What GE's CEOs exemplify is the ability to perform four seemingly contradictory tasks (a near-impossible quadrafecta):

- Produce good short-term performance regardless of how the markets and competitors buffet the company they've inherited.

- Deploy resources so that organizational capabilities improve in the medium term.

- Align the talents and energies of hundreds of thousands of employees with clear strategic objectives.

- Develop and modify those objectives over the long term so that strategy adjusts to the changing business environment.

This is a feat that simply cannot be done by a team. It can be pulled off only by an individual with a clear vision.

The job is inherently difficult—and becoming more so. CEO turnover is on the rise globally, and studies show that the proportion that can be traced to inadequate performance is steadily trending upward. Why should the job be harder now than in the past? I see two reasons. First, arguably, market conditions are making the task of getting good results harder. Hypercompetition, changing technology, and a raft of emerging players from every corner of the globe are pressuring companies to keep changing their game, and a lot of firms are just not doing it very well. When I took a look at the performance of U.S. firms over the last five years and discounted the top two firms from any industry, the rest, on average, failed to earn their cost of capital. Second, owner expectations have changed radically. In a world where markets are growing 5% annually, the stock market is looking for 15% returns. Institutions count for an increasing share of ownership, and their holding period is getting shorter—under a year is now typical. These are not owners so much as speculators in for the short ride.

Outsiders, Insiders, and Hybrids

When company performance disappoints, boards of directors tend to seek a white knight from the outside to come in and change everything. Most of the time, the only way to change things fast is to cut costs—which is exactly what someone unfamiliar with the specifics of an industry and its markets, or the company and its people, is likely to do first. Yet a study by Booz Allen reports that outsider CEOs who make a quick mark by cutting costs generally fail to succeed in the long run: After two or three early years of squeezing more to the bottom line, the CEO leaves or sells the company. This short-term orientation destroys value in the medium and long terms. The seeds of growth are eliminated along with overhead.

When a board looks inside for future leaders, all too often it sees men and women who don't seem to have the stature and vision to lead. In the board's view, they are good operators, but they lack a strategic sense: They have never run a business in anything like the circumstances that loom on the horizon. And where no systematic effort has been made to build future leaders, that perception may be correct.

But there's no better way to reverse the long-term destruction of shareholder value than for companies to commit themselves to growing executives from inside the company who are prepared to lead through good times and bad. Simple? No. The right thing to do? Absolutely.

Consider the four skills that a new CEO needs to drive a company forward and produce the results cited above:

- Judge where the world and the company's markets are headed, and frame a vision of how the company should reposition itself.

- Identify (and if needed recruit) the talent that can turn this vision into reality.

- Understand, in a deep and substantive way, the problems the company faces.

- Know, comprehensively, how the company really works—in other words, be plugged into its administrative inheritance and know key players well.

True, carrying out these tasks requires a clear outside perspective. Industries are regularly transformed by changes that disrupt traditional economic relationships. That's what the Internet did to the world of personal computers and minimills did to the big, integrated steel producers. It's what high-quality, low-cost Asian manufacturers did to a whole set of businesses based in Europe and the United States. Individuals with an outside perspective can see such trends as they're happening.

But three of these four leadership skills require extensive inside knowledge. Executives who successfully lead large corporations to new heights usually have accumulated a body of knowledge over a long span of time, much of which is specific to the company they're leading and the industry it's a part of. They can assess the talents of their colleagues relative to the skills needed to compete in a new situation. When, in response to a change initiative, colleagues declaim, "We can do that," insiders can distinguish wishful thinking from an accurate recognition of vital, new internal capabilities—and they can do so early on. It's hard to overstate how important it is to understand, when competing in a new field, the true value of recognizing a winning versus a wannabe capability.

My research suggests that as a rule the best leaders are, therefore, people from inside the company who have somehow maintained enough detachment from the local traditions, ideology, and shibboleths to maintain the objectivity of an outsider. They know the traditions and the people of the company but also know how those will have to change. They know what best-in-class looks like as well as how the class will change. They're able to look at the organization's administrative heritage as if they had just bought the company.

How do they preserve that view? Often they come from outside the mainstream of the organization. They've spent more of their time away from headquarters living with new opportunities and threats. If you've been living in modern Shanghai, for instance, you're aware that the threat from China is not cheap labor.

Am I advocating the elevation of eccentrics and misfits? Of course not. Procter & Gamble's A.G. Lafley spent the years before becoming CEO in Asia building the Chinese operation—in beauty products rather than the core and very mature P&G detergent business. His resulting broad view of P&G's potential may have laid the basis for the series of major acquisitions that have substantially widened the domain of the company's businesses. IBM's Sam Palmisano was a champion of software and open systems at a time when Big Blue was essentially a closed-system, hardware-oriented company. Again, his broader view of how IBM should compete appears to have shaped the company's progress as a systems and services solution provider. What Jack Welch built into a world leader was GE Plastics—not engines, lighting, or appliances (which were GE's core at the time). Welch once told me, "One of the things that I was lucky about in my early days in GE: I got good businesses and I saw bad businesses. I was managing diamonds—industrial diamonds—and semiconductors. So one of the advantages of being in a business with a 50% margin and moving to a business with a 4% margin is that you can tell the difference between the two, and you want to get rid of [the 4%] and keep [the 50%.]"

Being outside the mainstream does two things for a high-potential manager: It allows a certain detachment from the conventional wisdom to develop, and it keeps the manager from being cowed by a powerful CEO. As one CEO said to me, "Acorns don't grow well in the shadow of great oaks."

Growing Leaders

How do you build a pipeline of future leaders that includes inside-outsiders? It begins with recruiting from a diverse pool of individuals who are both highly talented in their area of specialization and have the potential to be general managers. Over time, they will learn to manage effectively in the context of the company's strategy, systems, and culture—they will become good insiders. The best of them will also see the potential for radical improvement, and that vision may ultimately match up with the sense the board and the departing leaders have of where the world is headed. Grooming that kind of insider—the one blessed with an outside view— should be the fundamental goal of the executive development process. If building the skills these managers need takes a decade or more—and if they are to assume leadership positions while they still have at least a decade of service ahead of them—they need to be on board and identified for grooming by the time they are 30.

"Grooming" may be a bad word for the development process, as it sounds more cosmetic than it really is. What high-potentials need is to be handed a series of increasingly complex assignments that give them the chance to manage a whole business as early as possible. That means the company has to be organized into more than one business unit—even if it is basically a one-business company. Sometimes regions are distinct enough to benefit from different managers. Western and Eastern Europe are like that today: One market is mature, highly developed, and very competitive; the other is growing rapidly under rapidly changing conditions. Thus managing them is quite genuinely two different jobs.

As high-potentials move through this series of increasingly complex assignments, performance evaluation is critical. They must be held accountable and learn how to deliver, but they must not be abused by arbitrarily imposed goals. When young managers stumble, they should be mentored by talented senior managers. This mentoring is part of the senior manager's path to further growth as well.

Senior managers who are overseeing the development of talented junior managers should pay special attention to planning, budgeting, performance evaluation, and compensation—and to how these different processes are linked. When managed well, planning and budgeting present an endless series of development opportunities: learning how to present deliverable plans so that they are not arbitrarily raised to meet some corporate aspiration; learning how to ratchet up growth while still delivering current performance; learning how to present new ideas in such a way that they are not underfunded. These challenges involve, on the one hand, being held accountable for deliverables and, on the other, being given space to nurture new activities.

Earning and learning require different approaches to evaluation and compensation. Both entail accountability, but one set of targets and measures is pretty clear, while the other is often more ambiguous. Rewards need to reflect each in a way that is understandable. An individual might be promoted for success in building an operation over a number of years, for instance, but at the same time be denied a bonus based on a formula related to short-term earnings.

Oftentimes, the inside-outsiders appear to present a special challenge. They seem like mavericks to the extent that they do see outside the box. What this comes down to is that most people think some of their ideas are really weird. Indeed, these unusual ideas may not be sound until they're worked through. Inside-outsiders need encouragement, as well as protection from old-timers who might be inclined to teach them a lesson. That is the job of the mentor.

The critical moment is when the young high-potential shows up with something new that just might be important. That is when the investment of a mentor's time is most important. It may take numerous meetings and a long walk or two to help the high-potential think through what it means to develop an idea in the context of the company. More often than not, the mentor will be at least as skeptical as the old-timer. The trick is to give the young manager the time and leeway to turn a new idea into a great business without giving him the rope to hang himself. The mentor must make sure resources are adequate but not excessive, dole them out stage by stage, and then wait and see. The mentor, in other words, is a kind of venture capitalist, teaching potential leaders how to make new ideas work.

It takes world-class quality and cost control for any company to stay in the game. It takes fast-to-market innovation to sustain industry leadership. Those dual (and dueling) priorities have put great pressure on the men and women at the top. They must drive efficient operations and creative change at the same time, even though from a management perspective those tasks are nearly contradictory.

For both the company leadership and those who seek to become leaders, that means balancing the need to meet short-term expectations with the need to invest over the long term in the development of the organization's people. For management, development involves giving potential leaders jobs with increasing responsibility. Helping them maintain their unique perspective takes hours of mentoring; protecting them from the consequences of their mistakes requires careful intervention. Those who want to be chosen as leaders must build a track record of delivering in the short term while building for the long term. Both challenges are tough, but both must be met if we are to restore our companies to long-term competitive health.

Becoming an Inside-Outside Leader

IF YOU WANT TO BECOME a company leader—and especially if you want to be an inside-outside CEO—you need to manage your own development from the start. These questions can help you keep the big picture in mind.

At recruitment

- Why are you being hired? Is it just for a job today, or is there a career path?

- Is this a company where talented people stay for many years? If not, will the experience it provides make you attractive to future employers?

- How will the company help you grow? What pattern of assignments will you get? Will you have time to learn?

- What kind of mentoring will you receive?

- What kind of training is offered? What is done in-house? What is done through outside programs?

- How soon can you run a business? If you don't get general management responsibility early, you can't learn the job.

- Is this a cookie-cutter program, or are young people given the chance to try out new ideas?

Now that you're on the job

- Do you meet your numbers?

- Do you help others? Are *you* developing their talent?

- What do you do for your peers? Are you just their in-house competitor?
- When you manage up, do you bring problems—or problems with possible solutions?
- Are you transparent? Managers who get a reputation for spinning events gradually lose the trust of peers and superiors.
- Are you developing a group of senior-manager friends who know you and are willing to back your original ideas with resources?

Developing yourself

- Is your network expanding outside your division? What about outside the company? Have you visited with customers, vendors, and related organizations? If you have a union, have you ever talked with its leaders?
- Do you know individuals in your community who aren't businesspeople? You can learn more about what you don't know from them than from people just like you.
- Do you attend seminars or expand your general knowledge beyond your immediate business?
- Are you involved with the community in some way? You can develop many leadership skills by working with an outside organization.

Living a balanced life

- Are you there for your family? Managing can be lonely—support of family can be invaluable.

- Have you cultivated a relationship with someone—spouse, close friend, mentor—who tells you the truths you don't want to hear? The higher you rise in your organization, the more your colleagues will tell you what they think you want to hear.

Originally published in November 2007
Reprint R0711E

About the Contributors

JOSEPH L. BOWER is the Donald Kirk David Professor of Business Administration at Harvard Business School in Boston. He is the author of *The CEO Within: Why Inside Outsiders Are the Key to Succession Planning* (Harvard Business School Press, 2007).

RAM CHARAN has been advising CEOs and boards of directors for more than three decades. His most recent books include *Boards That Deliver* (Jossey-Bass, 2005) and *Confronting Reality: Doing What Matters to Get Things Right* (Crown Business, 2004), coauthored with Larry Bossidy.

DAN CIAMPA is an adviser to senior executives, particularly during leadership transitions. He is the coauthor, with Michael Watkins, of *Right from the Start: Taking Charge in a New Leadership Role* (Harvard Business School Press, 1999).

EDWARD J. COYNE, Sr., is an assistant professor at Samford University's School of Business in Birmingham, Alabama.

KEVIN P. COYNE teaches strategy at Harvard Business School in Boston, Massachusetts and serves as a senior external adviser to McKinsey & Company.

KENNETH W. FREEMAN is the chairman and former CEO of Quest Diagnostics, the largest medical testing company in the United States. The company is based in Teterboro, NJ.

RAKESH KHURANA is a professor at Harvard Business School in Boston, Massachusetts.

JAY W. LORSCH is the Louis E. Kirstein Professor of Human Relations at Harvard Business School in Boston, Massachusetts.

NITIN NOHRIA is the Richard P. Chapman Professor of Business Administration at Harvard Business School in Boston, Massachusetts.

MICHAEL E. PORTER is the Bishop William Lawrence University Professor at Harvard University; he is based at Harvard Business School in Boston, Massachusetts.

MARGARETHE WIERSEMA is a professor of strategy at the University of California, Irvine.

Index